# BUILD
# TRUST

THE FOUNDATION FOR LASTING SUCCESS

ELEVATING LIFE, RELATIONSHIPS, AND BUSINESS

## RON BLACKBURN
## MIKE MOORE

Build Trust

The Foundation for Lasting Success

Ron Blackburn and Mike Moore

Copyright 2018 Vandalay Publishing

ISBN: 978-0-692-12115-3

All rights reserved.

This book features contributions from business people who model the principles in this book. Their contributions and support were fundamental in the development of this book.

Printed in the United States of America

# BUILD TRUST

# DEDICATIONS

**Ron Blackburn:**

I would like to dedicate this book to those who built the foundation of who I am today and have helped to significantly shape me along the way. I accredit my sense of humor to my mother, Cheryl, who taught me to laugh and make people laugh at all things in life, even when the timing may not be appropriate. To my father, Nick, who I grew up with, I learned to be thankful, the importance and pride that goes with being part of a family, and what it is like to give and receive unconditional love. From my biological father, Russ, I learned, or was maybe genetically predisposed to have, people skills, confidence, to question everything from a non-threatening position of curiosity, a continual willingness to learn, and that anything worth analyzing is worth over analyzing! To my brother, Kelly, I enjoyed laughing at everything with you, as well as learned to be humble and find the beauty in all people at an early age. To my sister, Renee, I enjoyed exercising our genetic over analyzation traits in people, feelings, and all social situations. To my wife, Lisa, who has allowed me to completely be myself, to spread my wings, to create new connections and relationships on a deep level that requires so much of my time, to entertain any idea or path that I feel needs exploring, to allow me to question anything and everything, to listen to my countless epiphanies, innovations, and inventions, which is exhausting, to say the least, and to trust the process, regardless how it may appear. To my daughter, Kelsea, whom I am so proud of and also so privileged to have in my life, the only person who gets to see me in my most uninhibited state, the most extreme silliness with no possibility of judgment, who I can laugh with until our faces hurt, who has joined me everywhere from black tie events to board rooms—she is the best thing that has ever happened to me and I mean it! To John Carter and Craig Dennis for their continual guidance, support, encouragement, inspiration, their willingness to talk and listen several times per day, regardless of their schedules or priorities. They are friends that no one deserves. To The Crew, who has given me, so late in life, a newfound hope. Thank you for helping me realize that the amount of time in which we know someone has nothing to do with the speed in which we connect or the depths of our relationships, when they are based on a pure intent. Individually we are strong, but together we are a force. We synergistically overlap our inspirational and experiential lives. They are the true inspiration for me wanting to write this book. They have taught me that everyone can build trust, build real relationships, and restore the way in which the world interacts with one another, elevating life, relationships, and business.

**Mike Moore:**

I am so grateful for the people who have loved me, challenged me, and held me accountable through the years. First, let me say thank you to my mother and father, Charles and Anne Moore, who made my life rich. They taught me the unconditional love of God in their words and actions and gave me a love of people, respect for human dignity, understanding of forgiveness, and a desire to always be learning, growing, and improving. To my wife, Susan, who has been a shining example of how people can be transformed by the renewing of your mind, I love you and am grateful for you daily. Thank you for challenging me to be a better man! One of life's biggest challenges is being a parent, and for all the joy my children, Chris and Stacy, have brought me, I am thankful! They have grown into exceptional adults who are committed to be their best and helping others be theirs. I love you both and can only hope and pray to be more like the people you have become. You always taught me so much and still are today! I also had the privilege of participating in the life of my stepson, Tanner Dufford, and in a time when his generation gets a bad rap, he continues to amaze me with his insights, understanding and, discipline. Watching all three of them and their families develop will make my life complete! To all of these people, I love you!

# ACKNOWLEDGEMENTS

**Ron Blackburn:**

I want to thank Greg Reid for giving me a glimpse into his world and then granting me full access. I don't know if he fully understands the exponential effect he is having on the world, as he has not just changed my life but everyone in my sphere of influence. Mike Moore, for allowing me to disrupt his busy life at such an interesting and seemingly inconvenient time, who trusted and allowed this creative collaboration, bringing a richer, fuller, and extremely experienced perspective on such a mutually passionate message. The journey was both educational and inspirational, and my life is better because of Mike. I would also like to express my sincere appreciation to those who have been instrumental in the development and creation of this book, those who demonstrate the traits in this book, and who create a culture of trust within their own circles, companies, and relationships. They have chosen to build trust first. I am proud to know each and every one of them and hope you, too, get the opportunity to meet them and experience their love, generosity, and willingness to give. William Marshall with Domestic Fab Design Studio, Corey Brushia with One Touch Living, and Larry Cerenzie with

FSC Coatings. To every customer, supplier, and sub who has helped me to learn, grow, and appreciate, you have molded and shaped me, and I am fortunate to have your trust and friendship. To everyone in the BIA of San Diego and to Karma International who truly embodies the spirit of trust, brotherhood, and camaraderie, I have learned from all of you. You know who you are, and I want to thank each and every one of you!

**Mike Moore:**

I want to acknowledge my father for coaching me from my earliest memories until the day he passed away and my mother for teaching me mental toughness. I also want to acknowledge the late John Wooden who took time to meet with me, mentor me, and share his thoughts on leadership, peak performance, and living life to its fullest.

Now for those who made this book happen! First, Ron Blackburn, the greatest builder of trust I have ever met, thank you! Knowing Ron makes me a better person and pushes me to new heights! To the others who made *Build Trust* a reality through their support and by inspiring me by being living and working as examples of the truths, natural laws, and love I believe in and teach. They've each chosen to build their lives and businesses on the premise that trust and the love of people are the foundation of all good things. Thank you for the examples you set for everyone who knows you, John Wallace of JW Flooring, Randy Wise of Randy Wise Homes, and Joe Lautner and Joe Roberts of Nortek. To every client and competitor who has helped me learn, grow, and improve, you have played a key role and I am blessed by your leadership, friendship, and being a part of the companies each of you have built in the construction, homebuilding, building supply, floor covering, and interior design industries. I have truly learned from all of you and want to thank each of you, and you know who you are.

# THE GREATEST GIFT

The greatest gift I have ever known is helping others learn and grow. As a mentor, author and speaker, I have dedicated my life and career to helping others succeed. Their successes, in turn, have become the key to my success. It's all about serving others, learning about their needs and dreams, and helping them make it happen.

The people I agree to coach, and mentor must be willing to learn, improve, and grow. I make sure they understand that success is not a destination, but rather a journey. They cannot expect success to come overnight—that is reserved for a mere handful of celebrities and musicians. In reality, I tell people that success is a process. Although the results might not be clearly evident right away, they must trust that by following the process, they will reap the rewards.

Ron Blackburn and Mike Moore are prime examples of this principle. Their careers and lives revolve around trust, and they know how important it is to have faith in the process. In the building industry, they know that the process begins long before they begin to build a home … it begins with laying a solid foundation of trust with each person they meet and every relationship they cultivate, whether it is with suppliers, employees, subcontractors, or their customers. When trust is established within their industry and community, they know it will be reciprocated and become an invaluable asset to their relationships and businesses.

Builders depend on blueprints to guide them through the building process. Those blueprints determine the ultimate finished product. *Build Trust* is the blueprint to building your business. Follow it, trust the process, and you will discover that the key to your success is also the greatest gift you'll ever know—helping others learn and grow.

*Greg S. Reid*
*Bestselling author, keynote speaker, and founder of Secret Knock*
*www.GregReid.com*

# INTRODUCTION

## Ron's Journey to Build Trust

I began in the building industry 41 years ago at the age of 13. My uncle got me into the industry to work summers and weekends during the school year. At such a young age, I didn't know what to do, so I looked to him for advice on everything. I trusted everything he said. I did everything he said. I was like a sponge, and I hung onto every word he told me.

He taught me the importance of asking questions of the guys that were older, experienced, and respected. He introduced me to them personally and then simply said ... do what they said. I found that the more I did what these guys said, the more they wanted to help me. It seemed to be such a simple rule that had mutual benefits to both parties, and I have carried this rule with me throughout my life.

I didn't understand mentor/mentee relationships or even know that there was a term for it until much later in life. I just knew that if I asked an expert for advice, they were more than willing to help, and when I took action on their advice, something magical would happen, an unusually rapid, real, and mutually beneficial relationship would be born, an exciting and rewarding relationship, of me wanting to impress the mentor and them wanting to see me succeed.

I used this secret everywhere I went. At 17, I attended the construction technology program at Orange Coast College. They had 27 slabs on campus. It was the largest and most specialized construction school in the nation. Every semester, they would build and disassemble 27 houses, teaching everything there is to know about the industry in the process.

I used this secret with all of my teachers. When I met my teachers, I would introduce myself to them on the first day. I would tell them that it was absolutely essential that I get an A in their class and if they could give me advice on how to do that, I would make sure and do everything they said. As a result, I got an A on every paper and every test. I started realizing that there was something more going on than just asking and doing. I had learned that out of these relationships I was forming, a foundation was being created that explained why everything was working so easily... That foundation was trust. When I did what I said I would do, trust was the result. Word started getting around that I was someone who could be trusted. I tried to introduce myself to new teachers after a few semesters and before I could finish, they would say, we know who you are. I got A's on all of my work. I received favoritism everywhere I went. I had mutually beneficial bonds with everyone around me that were real and based on trust.

Later in life, I learned that my secret could not be guaranteed to work every time. I had been fortunate for a long time, but there were people out there who would take advantage of my trust. I learned that trust must be qualified and cannot just be given blindly. I also learned that trust is fragile, can easily be broken, and rebuilding is much more difficult than building the proper foundation of trust in the first place.

Mike Moore is a person I trust. His willingness to share his expertise and wisdom is a perfect example of the secret I have described. This collaborative effort has exponentially and synergistically brought more value and enjoyment to the process, in addition to the end result. In this book, we will share with you guaranteed methods to achieve happiness and success, but they might not be what you expect. Not only will these methods and ideas get you where you want to go, but they will also allow you to enjoy the journey along the way!

## Mike's Journey to Build Trust

My human nature is selfish, and so is yours; this gets in the way of what's best for us. We are no different in this regard. If we don't overcome our nature, we don't build trust. It took me awhile to learn that what I wanted was often driven by my human nature to be selfish. In business, and in life, selfishness always sabotages our ability to build trust and do what's best for us.

I have been speaking, coaching, and consulting full time since 1992 and I have watched throughout my career as businesses made selfish intentions their core values. We have all experienced the results of businesses focusing on sales and profits, rather than service and adding real value to their employees' and customers' lives. Today, we have reached the breaking point with employees and customers not trusting the intentions of their companies or salespeople. Add to this that we are beginning to see Artificial Intelligence, yes, robots like Pepper from SoftBank, beginning to go to work in sales and the customer engagement. I began speaking about this over 25 years ago and challenging leaders and salespeople to shift their intentions to truly caring, helping, and serving their employees and customers. In 1995, I began teaching salespeople to make customers, instead of sales. This requires all of us to look at what's really best for everyone, instead of how to get what we want, regardless of how it affects others. I am now a believer in long-term selfishness, which means always doing what's best for others is what's best for me. So, I learned to channel my human nature by resetting my default short-term selfishness to a longer-term approach and discovered it also improved my immediate results.

In addition to my selfish human nature, I'm a recovering people pleaser, so if you can relate, there is hope for you, too. My early years in life and business were driven by my desire to be liked and accepted. One day in my early twenties, I took a phone call from a good customer, a homebuilder. He asked me if I could do something for him, and I said yes, as I always did as a people pleaser. Then, as I was hanging up, I thought, that's not right; it's not even the best thing for my customer. It was just easier to say yes. This time, instead of doing whatever it took to keep my promise, I called him back and said it wasn't even fair to ask me for that service. To my surprise, he said, "Okay, so what can you do?" I gave him an alternative, which was better for him, and me by the way, and he said, "Okay, let's do that." At that moment, I was set free and began only doing what was best for my customers, not just what they wanted, but what was truly best for them. My intention shifted from wanting to be liked and accepted to wanting to be a likable, trustworthy expert, who could help, serve, and always do what was best for the customer—even if that meant losing a sale. I was now focused on making customers, not just making sales, and my sales began to increase. As I taught this to others, their sales soared, and I am now an advocate for changing the dysfunctional relationship between companies and employees and salespeople and customers. It wasn't until I understood that pleasing people was a selfish intention that I could reset my intentions and start helping, serving, and always doing what's best for others that I could really start building trust!

I was no longer driven to please; I was committed to serve. Since that day, I've been doing business by trusting this process and have experienced the better immediate results, long-term relationships, and sustainable success. Be aware, though, that you can, and I have, given into my nature and damaged my relationships and results. Know this, I encourage you to check your intentions daily and reset them often or suffer the consequences of your human nature.

For all I had been blessed to learn growing up as a coach and teacher's son about how to help people become their very best, I could use my knowledge to its fullest until I understood my nature and shifted my intentions.

Today, I'm still learning how to apply these lessons to my personal relationships, where the intention to be liked and accepted can be even more dominant. I'm also aware our human nature doesn't change—we have to manage it daily and reset our default settings to be our best self and overcome our human nature.

I wrote this book with Ron Blackburn, who I found understood these principles and had become a trustworthy expert, to encourage you to trust the process that builds trust and encourage you to develop the courage to do what's best, not what's easy, so you can experience your highest self and the rewards that person will produce.

"We rise to our highest self while lifting others."

# CHAPTER ONE

# TRUST...
# THE MOST VALUABLE
# CURRENCY IN THE WORLD

C urrencies have recently dominated nightly news and social media debates as Bitcoin enjoyed a sudden and impressive hike in value, followed by a downturn that was just as sudden. People wanted a piece of the action as talks revolved around the possibility that this, albeit controversial to some, currency might be the currency of the future. Visions of wealth spurred many to invest in it, and some even speculated that Bitcoin would eventually be an international currency that would at minimum deflate the U.S. dollar, and at most, replace it.

We all know that the U.S. paper dollar used to be backed by gold but today is only backed by trust. Without trust, the paper that goes into our pockets and bank accounts would hold no value, and the money that is invested into our businesses would be worth nothing more than the paper it is printed on. It is what backs the money that has always been important and decides its value. It's always been that way, and regardless of the currency being discussed, that is not about to change.

In order for currencies to be sustainable, they must be backed by something ... or at least we used to believe that. With more than 1,300 crypto currencies currently being exchanged in the world, there is one currency that is worth more than all of them: Trust.

This might spur a significant question and one that is reasonable: Why would we consider trust to be a currency?

Like currencies, which must be backed by something, businesses must also be backed by something or they will be certain to lose value. Most entrepreneurs build their businesses with hard-earned money and sweat equity. The financial investment is often significant and usually what is attributed to be the biggest stake in their launch and success.

However, we propose that trust is a currency that is much more valuable than the almighty dollar. Businesses that are built on financial backing are vulnerable. The economy and the market will always impact their worth. In addition, when the funds deplete, they must be restored in order for the business to survive, let alone thrive. What happens, though, when trust is a business's biggest asset? Trust never depletes; it sustains its value or grows over time. Trust continually fuels the business, even in a struggling economy or when other currencies lose value.

Many businesses have suffered their demise at the fate of Wall Street! Factors outside of a business's control can cause entire industries to fail, and hardworking entrepreneurs who have invested their life savings into their business can stand by helplessly as their investment plummets in one fell swoop. But when trust is the backbone of a business, it is a currency that is not subject to outside factors. Trust is, in fact, the only currency that is totally within your control.

Let's look at it from another angle. Trust is the greatest marketing tool you'll ever know and the basis for nearly every referral a business will ever receive. It doesn't cost a dime, but it is priceless. Its value always increases over time, meaning it will never depreciate. Any currency can and will fluctuate in value. It will depreciate. It can be deemed weak, or at times, strong. However, when trust is your biggest asset and investment, its strength will not be called into question. Therefore, trust is the foundation every business should be built on. This is especially true in the building industry.

Trust is a marketing tool because it creates strong relationships. Whether that relationship is with a business partner, employee, or a spouse, trust is the foundation or thread that holds it all together. When trust is violated or breached, the fabric of the relationship will begin to unravel, severely weakening it until it eventually has little to no resemblance to what it once was.

We know that trust is critical to relationships and success, but we also know that trust is multi-faceted. It can mean different things to different people and that meaning can alter, depending on the circumstance or relationship. Some claim that success is the result of marketing, while others attribute it to quality or customer service. In relationships, we hear about characteristics like loyalty, faithfulness, and dependability. Under every definition, whether in relationships or business, there is one common factor that we don't often think about ... trust.

Unfortunately, for many, trust is a given. We don't think about it ... until it's gone. Trust is so vital to any relationship, yet its importance is never fully recognized until that trust is absent. That's because trust is the component that holds a foundation together. It's the currency that backs the entire organization. We automatically assume it's there or take it for granted, until one day when we are surprised to find that the foundation is falling. Scrambling to hold it together, we don't realize until it is too late that it is irreparable.

*I will trust you until I'm given a reason not to.* We've all heard, said, or lived by that rule at one time or another. But what happens when you are given a reason not to trust someone? You're hurt and angry, and the damage is not easily undone. It may take years to build trust, but a breach of trust can destroy a relationship or a reputation in a heartbeat. That's because trust is a basic need. It must exist in order for a relationship to be healthy. Businesses are not exempt. The relationships we have with partners, vendors, subcontractors, and clients depends on trust. When that trust comes into question, so, too, will the loyalty and cooperation of every individual who depends on it.

Maslow understood this, and in his Hierarchy of Needs he lists safety and security as two of our most basic desires. From infancy, we trust that those will be provided to us. As we grow older, they become critical in our relationships with friends, coworker, clients, relatives, and spouses. With something that important to our lifelong needs, it becomes even more vital that we establish trust first and foremost, rather than leaving it to chance.

Coaches understand this. Even with the same people on a team, spring training requires leaders to regain their core group of players' trust every single year. Each member needs to be reminded, through both words and actions, that they can trust their coach to have their best interests at heart, that they have the coach's support, and that the decisions made are with due consideration for every member of the team. Without that trust and its reinforcement every year, players will question the coach's motives and will not give them 100 percent of their effort or talent.

How do you build trust in a business? Building trust can start even before a business exists by building quality relationships. Organizations that have real relationships between leaders and employees, employees and customers, leaders and customers, and employees, leaders, and other individuals and businesses that serve the industry have more value and a far greater chance to flourish and succeed than organizations that lack trust within its walls and in the marketplace.

Relationships are a critical factor in building trust. We've all heard that word-of-mouth is the best advertisement. People prefer to work with people they know, like, and trust. If they don't know a reputable company, they'll turn to someone they do know and trust and ask them for a recommendation. It's a trickle-down effect—when you trust someone, you generally trust the businesses and people they trust.

With trust in place, all of the other most important qualities and behaviors of a business fall into place, naturally and without effort. Common obstacles and challenges become nonexistent as trust creates loyalty, teamwork and a genuine willingness to help, nonjudgment, and a real team effort to solve problems together without assigning blame. In addition, trust leads to a culture or environment that is filled with smiles and laughter, and when people enjoy what they're doing, it leads to stellar customer service. When you and your employees are happy, it will impact the relationships you have with clients and others in your network.

### Trust is Making a Comeback

Today, the core interest in sales is selfish. Most salespeople's primary intention is to make a sale and earn a commission. When your only intention is to make money, your intention begin to mirror those of a thief. Sure, profit needs to be made in order to maintain a business; however, the purpose of a business should be to provide real value to employees and customers. In turn, revenue will naturally be generated. However, the building industry (as well as many other industries) has been putting the cart before the horse for too long. Instead of providing real value and a service, which will then generate revenue, they focus on generating profits first, causing them to work backwards.

The almighty dollar cannot be our only motive. Mother Teresa knew this. She provided a valuable service to others. If she'd been in business with that intent, she would have generated an impressive income. Bill Gates is another example, as are other successful entrepreneurs. Steve Jobs said, "You have to start with the customer experience and work back to the technology, not the other way around." Peter Drucker said, "The purpose of business is to make a customer." The most successful businesses are built to provide a valuable service to others that creates a relationship between the customer and the business. Microsoft, Amazon, and Apple all provide services and products that help people, and those people are excited about doing business with them.

Making trust, service, and value a priority to customers is not a new concept. It is the way business was conducted 60, 70, 80 years ago. In those days, a simple handshake represented a man's contract and his word. That is a far cry from how business is conducted today. What happened? In the 1960s, business intent changed, and the focus found a new mark—money before value or service. There was a fevered push to increase sales and profits, while reducing costs. Speeding production resulted in a sacrifice in quality. We saw it in the manufacturing sector as plastic components replaced sturdier materials, and in sales, where the focus turned from serving the customer—a concept which we know as providing a solution, rather than a product or service—to making a sale. Numbers and quotas and the bottom line took precedence over people, service, or quality.

Such an about face in production and sales seeped into the building industry, as well. Building homes faster and cheaper became more important than providing the customer with what they wanted. Builders adopted the mindset that they know what the customer wants ... the customer does not. Don't believe it? When asked to finish the following, "Buyers are ...," the majority of builders (and realtors) will say that buyers are liars.

Builders and real estate agents don't trust buyers. Conversely, buyers don't trust builders or realtors. In this book, you will discover why. You'll also become aware of how much damage this has done to the building and housing industry—the only industry in which there are far more qualified and interested buyers than people who actually buy.

No business can thrive if it puts the seller before the buyer. The cart is in front of the horse, and it is time to right this wrong. We can no longer expect people to buy, then hope they trust us. We must make trust an integral part of our foundation, or we will place our livelihood and reputation in severe jeopardy. Trust should not be something that is given automatically. It has to come first. By building trust first, we will create a foundation that will sustain any turbulence thrown our way.

In this book, we propose a need to step back in time to a day when a person's handshake was his word, and that word was gold. We propose that by shifting your intentions to helping, serving, and always doing what is best for the customer, you will grow your business. Companies that are built on trust don't need elaborate written contracts and warranties. Like a handshake, their word and their reputations precede them. Customers know they will deliver what is promised, on time and within budget. When this happens, companies don't need gimmicks or marketing tactics. They don't need to shave every line item to strive to be the low bidder who gets the job. Their reputation is their bid ... it assures the customer that the company will be honest and fair, conscientious and proud of the quality they deliver. They know the company provided them with a realistic budget and timeframe, and neither will be exceeded. Open communication increases, and there is no need for excuses to appease the customer and salvage a reputation.

Trust can do all of that. When a company bases itself on trust, first and foremost, that trust seeps into every relationship. General contractors, subcontractors, suppliers, and external organizations, like insurance companies welcome that trust and strive to keep it. Trust becomes mutually beneficial to everyone in the chain, from the business owner to his/her employees, from the employees to the customers and vendors, and from the subcontractors to the tradesmen, who recognize that trust is their greatest asset and one they are not willing to risk losing.

What happens when trust is lost? Employees who don't trust their employers question their motives and lack security. Not surprising, this leads to a high turnover rate. Employees who don't feel trusted are less likely to be engaged in the business. They are not willing to go the extra mile and work together as a team to solve problems when they arise. Vendors and suppliers who don't trust a business may be reluctant to extend credit or go out of their way to adhere to tight delivery schedules. Prices and interest rates can increase, so not only does a lack of trust affect relationships, it also affects the bottom dollar and ability to meet deadlines within an agreed upon budget.

When businesses lose the valued trust of the community, its customer base, it will eventually lead to the demise of the company. Wall Street agrees—when a company's motives or actions come into question or are met with disapproval and public trust is lost, its values decline. We've recently witnessed the fallout that occurs when companies lose public trust:

- A video of a United Airlines passenger being physically removed from one of its places in 2017 resulted in a $255 million loss in market value for the airline.

- Toyota sacrificed quality control when focusing on expanding its marketing operations, resulting in hundreds of thousands of recalls and Congressional oversight due to their lack of focus on customer safety. This is similar to what happened decades ago when sales and profits took priority over quality—Toyota put the cart in front of the horse, and in doing so, they put their reputation at stake and suffered deep financial losses.

- Uber faced controversy in 2017, leading to the termination of its CEO and more than a dozen of the company's upper-level managers and executives. To rub salt in the wound, its blemished reputation caused a double-digit decline in applicants for positions within the company. People want to work for companies they can trust.

These are just a few examples among thousands that can be cited. Trust is an asset, and when it is called into question, there is a definite and measurable reaction. Some businesses survive, but usually only after enough time has passed that they can rebuild that lost trust. Unfortunately, some businesses cannot afford the luxury of time and cannot sustain the damage.

Because trust is so critical to a company's survival and bottom line, it is making a comeback—people not only expect trust, they are demanding it. The building industry is no exception. Homeowners have a lot at stake in a house. For most, it is their largest purchase and greatest asset. They want to know with as much certainty as possible that the company they hire is reputable, honest, fair, and trustworthy. Today's customer is educated. They do their homework and read reviews. They know that investing time in learning about a company before choosing a builder can save them a great deal of time, money, and frustration later.

The majority of the challenges builders face can be eliminated by investing in one thing—trust. Rather than building a business and investing in advertisements and marketing, try trust. Build trust first; the customers will come. People within the industry will turn to you. They'll seek and heed your advice. They'll trust that you will do what you'll say and say what you'll do. It's an investment in your reputation that will generate sales and revenue, while continually growing one of the greatest assets you and your business will ever know—real, quality relationships with those you meet, interact with and employ. Let's not forget the relationships with your customers! Trust is your greatest asset and currency, and happy, satisfied and loyal customers will be the revenue that are the foundation of your success.

You wouldn't invest everything you have in a currency that isn't backed by something. Don't make the mistake of backing your business with a currency that lacks credibility. As long as trust exists, it cannot depreciate or lose value. And that's the best currency a company can have.

At the end of this book, you will be introduced to living examples of people who build trust—people we have been honored and privileged to know. They are individuals who exemplify trust in everything they do. They embody the principles in this book, and their successes are stellar representations of the positive impact trust will have on your business and your relationships. Read their stories and let them serve as mentors who want to contribute to your growth and success. While trust is the most valuable currency you'll ever know, these role models are living representatives of its true value—their contribution to this book increases its credibility.

We commend them for being trust leaders and investing in the oldest and most valuable currency there is. Our relationships with them have proven that trust is the only currency that consistently appreciates over time and is mutually beneficial.

"Losses will happen along the way. Trust the process and you'll improve your results."

# CHAPTER TWO

# TRUSTING THE PROCESS AND THE POWER OF NATURAL LAWS

This book proposes shifting our intent from producing profit to producing trust. As they say in the movie *The Field of Dreams*, if you build it, they will come. If you build trust, the customers and clients will come. Trust will always attract customers better than prices, incentives, or marketing gimmicks.

Our natural inclination is to get the customer first and build a trusting relationship later. That requires some sense of blind trust, which for those who are skeptics, is difficult. However, it is imperative if you want to build, sustain, or grow your business in the building industry. Personally, and professionally, we both believe that it is better to trust first and be disappointed on occasion than it is to hold trust at bay or withhold it altogether.

Why trust first? There are several reasons. First, trust is the foundation of a business that makes people aware that they are important to you. By building relationships based on trust, you remove selfish intentions that make customers, in our case, homeowners and developers, seek us out. They trust us to do what is best for them and provide them with the highest quality service possible.

Your business does not start with a buyer. It starts with a person who is shopping for a home. They become a buyer when they sign a contract and only become a customer after they move-in and are happy enough to recommend you to others. You can't focus on the sale first; you have to start by treating them as a customer from day one. When you shift your focus from the buying experience to the ownership experience, you will begin to increase your sales.

Focusing on trust first requires trust. You have to trust that the process works. You have to trust that this method of building a business will produce results that will sustain your business. That is not natural for most who are vested in their business and naturally focused on the end result, and that makes it difficult for you to trust an outcome you cannot see.

If you find it difficult to trust the process, consider our natural laws. A natural law can be defined as something that is at work whether you believe in it or not. You either choose to trust that law and reap the benefits, or you ignore it and suffer the consequences because it's always at work. The natural law of trust works just as gravity does. You can choose to ignore it, but it will still be at work and either help you or crush you.

The common thread in those definitions is human nature. In order to understand why you should put trust first and trust that the process will work, it's important for us to understand human nature.

When seeking a first job or starting a new career, the common challenge people face is that they have no experience. But they cannot get experience without getting a job in the industry. It's a catch 22 that many have experienced. Trust works the same way—people are reluctant to hire a new builder because they don't know anything about them. They don't know if they're conscientious, reputable, or trustworthy. They have no idea if they deliver quality services or will do shoddy work. People have been burned in the past and they remember it well. For that reason, they turn to other people and ask them who they can trust. They have three bids in hand but don't know what sets them apart. Given that they are most likely to choose a builder who comes with excellent recommendations and high praises, doesn't it make sense that trust should be built before a sale is made? When no trust is built or found to differentiate the bidders, the low price is often the winner and buyers often lose.

Let's look at human nature from another perspective.

It is human nature to distrust someone who cannot maintain eye contact. In fact, studies have shown that said eye contact should last for a minimum of eight seconds in order to produce trust. People who are authentic and have a genuine concern for others make this eye contact naturally and the process of building trust begins. When people try to replicate this without a genuine intent to help others it eventual backfires and ends in mistrust.

The eight-second rule applies to another aspect of human nature. We decide to trust people in the first eight seconds of meeting them. In fact, 93% of conversation is nonverbal.

By 40 seconds in, it is almost impossible to change how you feel about that person and whether or not you trust them. The power of your intention screams at them in the first eight seconds! Now, that's not sufficient time to give your sales pitch or describe your business ethic. But it is enough time to convert a shopper to a buyer based on something that is intangible, but vital, to a healthy working relationship.

---

### Ron's Trust Story

Having recently moved and relocated my business, I needed customers. Rather than seeking projects and sitting at my desk pounding out bids as a new, but unknown name, I picked up the good old Yellow Pages and found the names of general contractors. I then called and arranged to meet with each one. Face to face, I looked them in the eye and told them about myself. In essence, I began to build trust to start new relationships with them before I expected or even attempted to win a bid. That gave me an advantage—I was no longer a strange name on a bid. Instead, I was a person they knew. They knew my motives and intentions. In the end, I submitted bids for their project and gained seven jobs.

---

It is human nature to remember the negative in life, and that can make people skeptical. On the other hand, it is human nature to want to work with people we like, know, and trust. The people we believe and trust the most are people we already know because we trust their intentions, but we will still watch to see if their intentions have changed and become selfish. Blind trust given in an existing relationship isn't even a good idea, which is why building trust isn't a one-time event but an ongoing focus to maintain good relationships.

Consider the fact that you wouldn't trust just any doctor or hospital with your heart. You'd do your homework first. You'd probably ask your general practitioner for recommendations on the best place to go or the best doctor to see, and his or her advice would be highly valued because you know that it is qualified by experience and knowledge. An educated review by an expert is irreplaceable but should never replace your own instincts for evaluating when to give trust.

On the same note, where do builders go when they need a new roof? They don't turn to bids; they turn to the most reputable and trusted roofing contractor they know. It's human nature.

Human nature works in much the same way as natural laws. We might not be able to see them, but we know they exist. We also have to overcome our nature and biases to be our best self. We cannot see gravity, but we do know that what goes up must come down. It has been proven and tested without fail—it will always be there and produce consistent results, regardless of anything we do or say.

Let's consider trust to be a natural law. Whether or not we recognize it, trust will impact every relationship and business transaction in every business. If human nature accepts that there are natural laws, regardless what we do or do not do, it stands just as true that making trust a priority in your business will always produce the best measurable results.

Just as the Law of Attraction produces a specific result based on one's thoughts and focus, trust also produces specific and measurable results. Like the Law of Attraction, the results are not known until they are produced, yet there is faith that those results will come. Trusting the process requires a similar sense of faith. While there is no guarantee that you will get the results, you're seeking with everyone you meet, history shows us that operating on the basis of trust is more likely to produce the best immediate results as well as create growth and the sustainable results.

People do, indeed, do business with people they know, like, and trust. The more people trust you, the more likely it is that they will share information with you. This information is a critical tool you can use to determine whether you are the right person for the job—instead of working from the flip side, when a potential customer is the one who makes that determination. Why is that important? According to *Forbes, Inc.,* if you are honest enough to turn down a potential sale, you don't lose a sale—you build a customer for life.

The reason for this is because you are operating from the right intent to help, serve, and always do what is best for people. Money is not your motive. You don't maximize short-term results with short-terms selfishness. Money is not the goal—instead, money is the result of trust. Mother Teresa didn't focus on money, yet she was astronomically successful in changing lives. Money is a short-term selfish intention. By maximizing the intent to help, serve, and do what is best for the customer, the end result will be more profit, more revenue, and more sustainable growth in business.

It is said that when you give, it will come back to you. As it turns out, your motive matters as much as your actions. However, when you give to receive, you really aren't giving, you are investing. When you give, it is done unconditionally as a way of life and that life will produce more than any investment can return. Giving as a way of life happens most often when you trust the law of trust. You'll never know where the return will come from, but it will come. However, our human nature wants easy, comfortable, and instant gratification. We have to focus on resetting these default settings every day. Every industry will require effort, sometimes doing things that you don't want to do, that make people perform better. Professional athletes know this—they know they have to practice, eat right, and maximize their strength, wellness, and physical potential to be the best they can be. You must do the same with building trust in order to be the best you can be.

The word trust, in and of itself, requires faith. You don't know when you'll get the result you want, but they will come. Investing in relationships produces results, maybe not in the way you anticipated. You may invest heavily in a relationship and build a great deal of trust with a person who will never become your customer. However, that person can introduce you, as someone they know and trust, to two or three people who want to build a home. That person may be the connection or the referral that opens doors and provides reassurance to investors, agents, contractors, and other affiliates who will play important roles to you and your business in the future.

Farmers know that they cannot harvest a crop unless they plant seeds. Not only do they have to plant them, but they also have to tend them, fertilize and cultivate them, nurturing them until a crop is produced and ready to harvest. That farmer knows that they cannot harvest a crop if they haven't bothered to plant a seed. The same holds steadfastly true for relationships, especially in business. You cannot attract and build a strong customer base unless you have planted the seed of trust. Then you must fertilize it, water and feed it so it will grow into a rich, rewarding, and healthy business.

If you focus on a tree for 24 hours a day, you won't improve the harvest. If you work every day to nurture that tree, though, you will reap the harvest you desire. Everybody focuses on the results without focusing on what is necessary to get them. The building and housing industry works in reverse. There has been a long trend to focus on the sale — winning a bid and getting a closing. But we've forgotten that we have to plant the seed before we reap what we sow. We're expecting customers to come out of the woodwork, looking for us, when that goes against the laws of nature. We must be the farmer who plants the seed and works the field that creates the crop we want.

Yes, this requires faith. Trust is a faith-based asset, much like natural laws that work, whether we believe in them or not. Trust removes selfish motives and makes helping people more important than the instant gratification of a sale. Yes, it requires discipline to stay on track, especially when we don't get the results we want as fast as we want them. By nature, we wake up as human beings with the desire to be as comfortable as possible, not to improve. The end result is that we are in an endless pursuit of the latest greatest diet and fastest, easiest fitness program. In the long run, though, isn't it best to do what is best for us in the beginning, rather than attempting to undo what our selfish actions have created?

The selfish intent to make a sale without building trust requires a lot more work, effort, and time than building trust before pursuing a sale. If you focus on the results, you won't get them. You won't win a game by focusing on the scoreboard. They focus on what is best for them and the play that's before them. They know they cannot win if they don't execute with the proper attitude, skills, and action. Looking at the scoreboard and focusing on a win puts the cart in front of the horse. The game must come before the win.

Vendors, suppliers, and manufacturers cannot accomplish their goals when they put the cart before the horse. The money cannot come before the customer. That means that people and relationships must always come first. Top salespeople know this—they know not to focus on quotas and numbers. They focus instead on helping people, serving them, and doing their absolute best for the customer. The best salespeople are order takers. Yes, order takers—they build trust that causes people to do business with them. They know that when they focus on the *method*, not the results, the money, the sales, will take care of itself. They know that they have to learn, grow, and improve, which are the three things that will improve their results. Those are the things that will impact other people.

Do you trust the natural laws that are at work? Do you trust your best to be good enough? Do you trust that you need to keep learning, growing, and improving? Before you ask anyone else to trust you, do you trust your own intentions to be best for you and your company? Do you trust the process to be best for you?

By focusing on helping others and being fair, reputable, and someone others can trust, you put people first and the results last. Your priorities shift, and when that happens, the universe and laws of nature begin to shift with them. The main component in building a business that is people oriented, not results oriented, is trust. Be someone others can trust. Be a business owner your employees will trust. Be a friend, advisor, and connection others can trust.

You wouldn't intentionally build a business on empty promises, missed deadlines, and false estimates. You wouldn't intentionally build a business on unhappy employees and unsatisfied customers. You wouldn't build a strong reputation within the industry on poor reviews, either. Many businesses have tried and failed because they lacked the components necessary for long-term sustenance and growth.

Your intent should be on people, not profits. Help them and serve them, regardless if they are potential customers or new employees. If you build a business foundation on trust, they will come—people will want to hire you. They will want to work for you and with you when you serve without selling. In the next chapter, you will learn why selling doesn't work ... and how you can utilize human nature to become a top salesperson without selling a thing.

"Selfish intentions never produce positive results."

# CHAPTER THREE

# THE MYTH OF SELLING AND THE MESS IT'S MADE

## *The Dysfunctional Buyer-Seller Relationship*

People don't like, trust, or believe salespeople, and salespeople don't believe prospective buyers tell them the truth. This is the condition of the buyer and seller relationship that exists today. No one would have started out to create this intentionally, but the intention to make a sale and money has made this happen. The intention to make a sale stands in the way of the ability to build trust. Therefore, we often ask for advice about purchases from our friends and family who we trust but are not qualified to give us the advice we are looking for. The sad truth is that those who we should be asking, the people who are selling us the products or services that we desire, are most often not trustworthy because we know their intent is to make a sale. We feel we are being manipulated, taken advantage of, and, frankly, know they care more about what's in it for them than about what's best for us.

The average customer doesn't feel important to a salesperson, and they certainly don't believe that salespeople are prone to offering the best advice or operating in their interests. After all, their livelihood depends on making sales and even more so when commissions come into play.

Have you ever been in the market to buy a car and been excited to see the salesperson scrambling to put on their suit jacket in the race to "assist" you? Probably not, and for good reason. You know what's coming. The inevitable sales pitch and the high pressure that comes with it. You might already know what vehicle you want and how much you can spend … but your armor immediately goes up because you also know that the salesperson isn't going to make this easy or painless. The car salesperson has you cornered. You're in their territory now, and they're not going to let you go until you've signed on the dotted line. Like a hungry animal about to pounce on their prey, you can almost see them drooling. In fact, sales trainers have taught salespeople to be hunters … This has instilled the wrong intentions and damaged the buyer and seller relationship!

In people, such behavior can be likened to thievery. Does that sound a bit bold and over exaggerated? We don't think so. A thief wakes up every day with the intent to make money. It doesn't matter how they do it or how much it hurts other people, as long as they get the job done.

You see, as long as making a sale or making money is your ultimate goal, your intentions will be off-putting to the buyer and they will feel you are no different than a thief. If profits come first, you communicate that you don't care about people or what you are able to do for them. Your main priority and concern is what they can do for you. You go from one profit to another profit, and instead of making customers, you make sales, but won't even make as many sales with these short-term intentions.

Not all salespeople have these poor intentions, but the vast majority do, and buyers hold all salespeople to be guilty until they prove themselves innocent. This can only happen when they make building trust and doing what's best for the buyer more important than the sale.

What happened? When did "sales" become a dirty word and a profession that's met with so much disapproval?

Up until the 1950s, companies focused on providing quality products and services. Brand names were trusted, and customers were loyal as the day was long—and rightly so, businesses and employees took pride in their work and invested in innovation that benefited the customer, not just profits.

Then, the 60s arrived, and with the new decade came a new business trend—companies stopped building better products in order to be better than the competition. Instead, they focused on ways to design and manufacture products faster and cheaper. Saving expenses was the mantra that dominated the manufacturing world, but it was at the customers' expense.

When the intentions changed from giving the customer the best experience to producing more profits, there was no longer a need to produce better goods and services. Businesses competed on a different level, by cutting costs even more. Profit, not quality, culture ensued among companies, one that trickled down not only to the customer, but also to employees who found that they were being viewed through the lens of profit, as well—how could they do more in less time to emphasize or increase the company's profit?

In a nutshell, what really happened was that companies adopted a selfish intention—to maximize their return, even if it meant sacrificing the quality that customers valued and the loyalty that their employees had established. It sabotaged the trust that major companies had spent years, even decades, building. It's a fact that as soon as we start taking advantage of customers, it damages employee relationships. Employees began to see themselves as overworked, underpaid, and replaceable.

As decades have passed and businesses have mastered maximizing profits, their marketing had to shift. People already knew that they were nothing more than a sale to these companies, so businesses had to switch tactics. Few are the advertisements that relate how a business is great or better than the competition. Instead, the focus is on getting customers to flock to them in other ways—using celebrities and marketing strategies that appeal to the emotions, usually those of instant gratification, to potential buyers.

Businesses are selling people, but people are waking up and they're no longer buying it. While salespeople are steadfast in their belief that they know better than the buyer, buyers have found their voice and are increasingly seeking to do business with companies they can trust. Apple recently experienced negative publicity and public backlash when it they admitted that a software patch intentionally slowed down older iPhones. Customers were upset. Some speculated that Apple had an ulterior motive—to entice customers to upgrade their phones. Others experienced frustration over their phone's battery life, and some invested in new batteries and, yes, new phones. While Apple stated that the software patch was actually meant to save battery life on older phones, the fact that they waited for nearly a year to reveal what they had done left some customers in doubt. The trust and loyalty Apple had earned from millions could have been jeopardized. Most customers would have understood if the company had disclosed the information right away. In the end, Apple gave the customers what they thought they wanted by slowing down their phones, rather than what they expected, which was a device that worked when they needed it. It was a scene out of the "we know what you want and what you need better than you do" playbook that offended customers.

In the homebuilding industry, it is actually common for salespeople to believe that buyers are liars. Buyers and sellers both don't trust each other. When you are at such vast odds, it is impossible to come together and maximize revenue, profits, and employee and customer satisfaction … and nobody wins.

Gone are the days when a builder quoted a price and stuck to it, even if it meant losing profit. Gone are the days when builders made quality their number one priority. And sadly, gone are the days when builders worked with their customers to find out what they really want and then did everything in their power to serve them in the best way possible.

It's time to put the present-day myth of selling to rest and bring back the forgotten, but once valued, customer from the dead. We've been doing it wrong for years. Let's consider this proposition: Everything that is of value comes from doing what you won't want to do. After all, isn't it reasonable to assume that most things that feel good are self-sabotaging or self-destructive and the best things for us make us uncomfortable?

Due to the same premise, the process most people use to find and choose a contractor or builder doesn't work. Quality service has taken a respite, as has trust, for years. Instead of building a business and customer base on the character of our business and an admirable purpose, we took the easy way out. Removing the human factor, the bid process has prevailed. Builders and contractors don't even have to meet homeowners anymore. There is no need for human interaction—that is, until something goes wrong. People decide what they want and invite contractors to submit a bid, providing the cost and details necessary to get the job done. We all know how it works. Usually, the builder with the lowest bid gets the project. Dollars and decimal points are given the highest priority … then a homeowner is surprised when they don't get the quality they believe they deserve.

Don't misunderstand—we firmly believe that homeowners deserve quality—especially when building their biggest and most expensive asset. But we've been going about it the wrong way.

## Why Three Bids Doesn't Work

As a society, we've mastered the art of convenience. We shop for cars, furniture, clothing, and even groceries online. We do our banking online and use apps to pay our bills. Convenience has a time and a place, but it has replaced the human factor. People no longer need to see products or meet business owners and their employees. A website has taken place of a first impression, and the customer experience is based on whether it is user friendly, not on any interaction with those in the business.

The bid process is similar. Builders review specs and blueprints and prepare an estimate, or bid, stating their fee for constructing a home or building. The first thing the customer looks at is the bottom line—how much is this going to cost ... and which builder is going to save me money?

The problem with choosing a builder based on price alone is that nowhere in that bid is there any indication of the quality of work that will be done. The homeowner cannot ascertain if the builder will, indeed, meet deadlines or provide quality materials and craftsmanship. And what if there are changes to the specs or unexpected delays? How will that be handled? And here's a big one—does the builder have a good working relationship with the subcontractors, the plumber, the electrician, the carpenters, the bricklayer, the roofer, and everyone else who has to work together in a very detailed, organized timeframe to keep the project moving and complete it on time? There are many factors to be considered when choosing a builder, especially when a home is your largest investment. There are even more things that can go wrong. Let's take a look at a few.

- Materials are not ordered on a timely basis, setting back all of the trades and extending the deadline of the project.

- Suppliers are not paid on a timely basis.

- Subcontractors and tradesmen may not be paid and refuse to report to the job site.

- A builder or general contractor is not available to troubleshoot issues or answer questions, thus causing delays and increased costs due to down time.

- Substandard work needs to be redone.

- The homeowner is nickel and dimed as costs exceed the bid, resulting in continual increases in costs.

This list can go on. Unfortunately, there are times when it does. That's why the bid process doesn't work. It doesn't provide the homeowner with reassurance that the builder is reputable and will, indeed, deliver on site what is reflected on paper. Frustration with the process can mar the customer's experience and create a strong sense of distrust with the builder.

It doesn't have to be that way. Buyers know what they want. They do their homework. They trust their builder to offer them advice when needed, and they also trust their builder to be professional, proficient in the industry, and fully committed to providing them with the services that are expected.

The only thing a bid tells you is the estimated cost for building a home. Nowhere on that bid is there any indication of how much experience the builder has, what their reputation is in the industry, the quality of their work, their relationship and demeanor with other workers and their customers, or their commitment to deadlines. They've never met the builder or learned their core values. To a homeowner, the builder is just a number on a page.

The bid process poses problems for builders, as well. The most qualified builder might not get a bid if their estimate is slightly higher than a substandard builder. Builders are well aware of this, so they look for innovative ways to shave costs and reduce their bids to a competitive level. Naturally, this can result in less time and attention being devoted to detail and craftsmanship, lower grades of materials and supplies, and the need to use less experienced subcontractors and tradesmen. In the long run, any one or all of these can impact a builder's reputation.

We're not selling our service and experience. We're guilty of selling for profit. Of course, we need to make a profit if we're going to continue to help and serve homeowners. But it should never be our ulterior motive. Getting a job at any cost can be costly, and it's not worth the ultimate sacrifice in the reputation a builder has at stake.

It's time to focus our businesses on people, not numbers. Like so many other industries, we've made a mess of the selling process. We've forgotten the customer and the pride in our work that inspired us to do what we do. We've forgotten that the most important asset we have is our employees. We've forgotten that there is one thing much more important than getting a bid, and that is building positive, trusting relationships with those we meet and serve.

What would happen if we scrapped bids for a moment and focused on building relationships before we build houses? From personal experience, people will develop trust in you and seek your opinions and advice. They'll refer you to those they know when they want a builder ... and that referral comes with a personal review of your character and your skills. When a relationship is established, homeowners will already know who they want to build their most important asset, and they won't need three bids. They will trust that your estimate is fair and honest. They will be confident that their builder is the right person for the job because they know what you stand for and who you are. In short, you won't have to sell yourself or your company. When people are more important than profits, trust supersedes price.

The trend has shifted. People are looking for a builder they can trust, not a salesperson with visions of dollar signs in his head. When you're selling, you're not doing your business or potential buyers a favor. But when you're serving and building relationships based on mutual trust, those buyers become something much more valuable—they become customers. In the next chapter, you'll learn the difference and how it can transform the way you do business forever.

"How you treat others doesn't reveal how you feel about them; it exposes how you feel about yourself."

# CHAPTER FOUR

# MAKING CUSTOMERS
# VS.
# SELLING

As previously mentioned, the intention to make a sale damages the buyer and seller relationship. So, what should our intention be if we want to heal this relationship, increase sales, and grow a business? It should shift from making a sale to making a customer. Let's define this more deeply. A customer is someone who owns and loves your product and trusts you to help others do the same. To make customers we need to become likable, trustworthy experts who care more about helping the customer than they do about making a sale.

Selfish sales intentions are precisely why people cringe when they think of a salesperson. Salespeople often believe that buyers are liars. This happens because in the traditional selling process, buyers don't open up and share honestly with salespeople because they don't believe salespeople have their best interest at heart. We need to get this straight before we go any further. A good relationship between buyers and sellers happens when we respect the buying process more than the sales process. When the salesperson's intentions are to help, serve, and always do what's best for the buyer and their purpose is to make a customer, not just a sale. Then, and only then, will the buyer invite the salesperson to be their trusted guide in their buying process. When this happens, the buyer opens up and begins to move forward in a conversation that allows a salesperson to help them.

When the salesperson is armed with a script that is designed to convince even the most skeptical and reluctant buyer that they absolutely need to buy and buy now, the selling begins. When the conversation shifts away from the script, they quickly bring it back, pointing out just why their product or service is bigger, better, and just what the customer wants — even when it's not. This sales process makes all salespeople look, sound, and act the same. The art of persuasion makes people retract. When a salesperson's purpose shifts to making a customer, the engagement becomes a conversation focused on serving the buyer. It revolves around the reasons for buying and changes how the buyer views and, therefore, interacts with the salesperson. When the salesperson focuses on what's truly best for the buyer, the buyer can begin to trust the salesperson and open up and share honestly what they really want. This engagement will always end in the buyer making the best decision for them and the salesperson making a customer, even when they don't buy that day.

Here's a great example. A couple visits a showroom, looking for flooring. They openly inform the salesperson that they can't afford top-of-the-line flooring and are looking for something affordable and within their budget. The salesperson knows that if he doesn't provide them with a floor that beats or meets the competitors' prices, the couple is likely to purchase their floors elsewhere. With the sale being the sole priority, the salesman pulls out their least expensive flooring and begins to talk it up, even though he is well aware that it won't be the best decision for the couple.

On the other hand, there is the salesperson who spends a considerable amount of time telling the prospective buyers why they should invest only in the flooring that will be best for them, even though it's been made known that they cannot afford it. The company has provided incentives for the highest sales of this particular brand, and the salesperson is motivated to earn that bonus. Still, it doesn't meet the homeowners' budget or have the particular look or performance they really want.

Who is right? Neither salesperson is right here. They both are focused on making a sale and not serving the buyer by doing what's best for them. One is willing to sell a low-quality flooring to them and risk the buyer's dissatisfaction with the look and wear of the flooring down the road. The other salesperson is aiming to sell a particular product, even if it's not in the buyer's best interest. Neither is focused on making a customer, just a sale.

What should these salespeople do in this situation? We propose that salespeople who make customers, always act in the best interests of the buyer. They will care about the buyer and stay focused on their ownership experience and not the transaction. They'll provide the customer with options, honestly disclosing the advantages and disadvantages of each. The salesperson should trust that when the buyer is informed with all the information, then and only then, can they help the buyer make a decision that is best for them. Top salespeople who make customers, not just sales, trust their buyers to make good decisions. This is a defining difference between customer makers and salespeople. And, salespeople who make customers end up making more sales. In fact, they end up building a customer base that buys from them often and refers others to them regularly. The best salespeople, who make customers, truly become order takers who are just doing what's best for their customers. They exit the buyer and seller relationship all together and become the trusted advisor who is always busy taking orders. Yes, we said it, the best salespeople become order takers. That's what building trust does for them and their company, it grows a sustainable business.

Customer makers manage their intentions and purpose to never allow selfishness to overtake them. They take into account so much more than a sale and work to make sure the customer will be even happier with the ownership experience than they are with the buying experience. So, making the ownership experience more important than the buying experience improves both and increases sales.

Here is another scenario. A man enters a car dealership looking to trade in his older two-door sedan. He tells the salesperson he's in the market for an SUV, something larger that will accommodate their newborn daughter. But his eye catches a sleek fire-engine red sports car on the showroom floor. He walks around it, feels the plush leather seats and opens the door. Before long, he's convinced himself that this car was made for him. The salesperson sees what's happening. Although he knows the sports car is not feasible for the man, he can taste the sale and the commission. Who is he to decide what the buyer needs or wants? His job is to sell him what he wants, right? Wrong. The salesperson is focused on the selling experience here, and his intention is not to help the buyer, but to make a sale. When it's all said and done, he might just make that sale; however, he won't earn the buyer's loyalty. And he might even be an accessory to a divorce proceeding!

That example might seem extreme, and admittedly it is. What happens when the buyer thinks they want something that is not best for them? Is it reasonable to try to sell a family of six a two-bedroom home? No, when you make a commitment to making customers, you are willing to walk away from a sale if, as an expert, you know the buyer's ownership experience won't be a good one and they will not end up a customer.

There are numerous ways a salesperson can breach a customer's trust. For the sake of making a sale, a salesperson might push the sale of a marble kitchen countertop to a couple with small children, without disclosing the fact that orange or grape juice spills will stain marble. In the end, the sale might happen, but the customer will probably regret the purchase. This won't happen when you make the ownership experience more important than the sale.

Another great example is found in the production home

building industry. New homebuyers state their number one reason for buying a new home is to personalize it before they move in. New homebuilders would rather they do all this after they move in because it's easier for them, but that's not what the vast majority of new homebuyers want to do.

Remember, to make customers you have to stay focused on the ownership experience, not the buying experience or ease of execution for the company. The vast majority of new home builders struggle with the personalization process because they just want to get the home built, closed, and move the customer in. If they start with the ownership experience and work back to the house, they would create an environment and process that could sell more homes and be sold out for 12 to 18 months in advance, while improving the homebuyer's satisfaction and their reputations. Now that would build a brand!

Selling to make a customer carries with it a responsibility to advise the customer when a purchase might conflict with their lifestyle or needs. Anytime you decide to sell someone something you know isn't best for them, you have sold out and will not make a customer. To make customers, be open, honest and direct. If you know something won't work, you should expose it, and never agree to do it ... in the end, the customer will thank you for saving them from making a costly mistake.

As a builder, you've probably met a homeowner who wants something particular—let's say a large two-story library with a sliding ladder. Do you agree, simply because it is what the customer wants? Or do you care enough to learn the reason for the library? This is a true scenario, and when asked if they read a lot, the homeowner admitted they do not ... but someone successful who they admired had a similar library. To the homeowner, it represented success and achievement. However, after discussing their reasoning and lifestyle, the homeowner decided to spend their money where it will get more use and bring them more joy. They love to barbeque and entertain, so they were excited to invest their money to enhance their lifestyle by making their outdoor space an amazing experience.

It's all about caring. Sure, this concept requires that builders spend a significant amount of time building trust, so homeowners value their opinion and insight. That is time well spent, allowing you to learn more about your customer and give them what they really want and within their budget. Can you see how futile it really is to bid a set of plans for house without first having a conversation with the customer? If you bid any project without establishing a relationship based on trust and your valued experience, your customer will not be happy with the final result. On the other hand, when you care and know your customer and they trust your advice, they will be happy, and you'll have a friend and a customer for life. If that's not enough, think about the exponential referrals that will be yours for years to come.

As builders, our job is not to sell to our customers. At minimum, those customers will regret that we didn't speak up and offer the advice and wisdom we've gained from experience. However, consider the same customer and how happy they will be when we approach them with the customer experience. By learning about them and offering them options that are in their best interests, we provide a valuable service that makes their lives easier … and they'll thank us for it.

However, most builders and salespeople in any industry believe that the selling experience is most important. Again, the cart is in front of the horse.

It was once believed that the purpose of a business is to make a customer. Business owners went out of their way to provide better services, better products, and better experiences for their customers. Those days are as long gone as the typewriter and black and white TVs outfitted with "rabbit ear" antennas. Today, there has been a gross shift and the purpose of a business has done a 180-degree turn— in today's competitive business climate, the purpose of a business isn't to make a customer—it's to make a sale.

But there's a problem—buyers instinctively know when they're perceived as a sale, not a person. They know when a salesperson cares about them and what's best for their needs … and they know when a salesperson doesn't care at all.

Well, here's a tip. As a builder, you're selling people on what you do. However, people don't buy *what* you do. They buy why you do it.

You only need to look as far as Tom's Shoes to validate that fact. Tom's has two mottos: "one for one" and "a purchase with a purpose," both of which are based on Tom's Shoes philanthropic and charitable donations. For every pair of shoes sold, Tom's donates a new pair of shoes to a child. The company also provides other services and donations to more than 70 countries across the world. People don't buy Tom's Shoes—they buy the lifestyle and the purpose behind the shoe. The fact of the matter is people know they can buy shoes anywhere. There is no shortage of establishments that sell shoes, even shoes are that are compatible to Tom's Shoes. But that's not the point—when people buy Tom's Shoes, they aren't buying shoes—they're buying why Tom's founder, Blake Mycoskie, sells shoes—to help and serve others.

This principle does not apply solely to products and services. How about ideologies and principles? Causes? Missions? Martin Luther King, Jr., had a dream, and millions supported his cause. They didn't care how he went about selling it, but instead were "sold" on why. Today, the late Martin Luther King, Jr., is a legacy and an icon, and his dream has outlived him and is still attracting followers and supporters.

Blake Mycoskie and Martin Luther King, Jr., built movements, not products or services. Their undeniable success cannot be attributed to a sales script or a salesperson's relentless drive or charisma. No, their entire success can be credited to one thing—unselfish intent. Their focus has never been to sell, but instead to help and serve people.

There is a vast difference between selling and creating a customer. Here's a good example:

Mrs. Smith has been a faithful XYZ customer for more than a decade. It's her go-to place whenever she needs a coat, clothes, or even items to upgrade her home. The salespeople know her well. They know what she likes and love helping her find what she needs. Mrs. Smith enjoys the customer experience so much that she won't shop anywhere else. Except she has one problem—she has difficulty finding footwear that fits her comfortably. One day, she expresses that to her favorite salesperson, who immediately suggests a shoe store across town—"They'll have what you're looking for. Tell them I sent; they'll take care of you."

Well, Mrs. Smith visits the shoe store and, lo and behold, they carry shoes that fit her feet comfortably and provide her with just the right amount of support! She buys two pair and walks away a satisfied customer.

Did XYZ lose a sale? Maybe. But they gained something much better—a customer—a lifelong, loyal customer. Now, whenever Mrs. Smith encounters a friend who needs something, she tells them to go to the XYZ store—she even tells them to ask for her favorite salesperson. "She's the best. She'll help you with anything you need. And if she doesn't have it, she'll tell you who does. I guarantee she won't steer your wrong."

Unfortunately, unselfish service like this is the exception, not the norm. As businesses turned their focus on generating more revenue and profits, not on adding value to the customer, this level of trust and customer service was swept to the wayside. In the coming age of Artificial Intelligence, the end of salespeople as we've know them is upon us. The only way for people to compete with the AI will be to truly love and care for their customers. Companies stopped building products and shifted toward faster, cheaper production. Serving the customer and doing the right thing became a thing of the past.

To better understand the differences between making customers and selling, selling is about presenting information about your product or service and making customers is about helping people improve their lives. Selling is about you, your company, and your product. Making customers is about how you can help the buyer do what's best for themselves. To make a customer, you'll need to be trusted enough to become the buyer's advisor, and that can only happen when you set aside the transaction and trust that if you help enough people get what they really want, you'll make more sales than any other way.

In a recent Gallop poll, entitled Honesty/Ethics in Professions, it revealed that only 21 percent of people trust real estate agents. More surprising, realtors ranked even lower than attorneys when it came to trust. While many factors can be attributed to these results, it cannot escape our attention that realtors are being viewed as salespeople with selfish intent (in this case, to make a commission). In fact, comments validate this, stating that many people believe real estate agents have one goal and that is to create wealth. Real estate agents neglect to build long-term relationships because a seller-buyer relationship in their industry usually ends at the closing. People simply don't buy or build houses on a frequent basis, so when the transaction is over, so, too, is the relationship.

Builders are also guilty of adopting this mindset. There is no need to build trust or a long-term relationship because the relationship is short-term. Instead of giving the customer what they want, providing quality and value to their lives, they focused on a quick turnaround at the lowest cost, with the highest profits ... get 'er done and get to the next one. The more we build, the more we make. New homebuilders celebrate the closing date in their process, and this is the date the buyer becomes a customer. So, only until homebuilders can focus on the ownership experience (that happens only after closing) will they begin to be trusted and make customers. This is also how they will create a brand that will increase their sales.

Selfish intent will always, *always,* sabotage trust. As soon as we start to take advantage of the customer, we damage the relationship that keeps our business alive. After all, without satisfied customers, we cannot sustain our business. We're biting the hand that feeds us, and then wondering why our business isn't booming.

What if we built trust and became the guide to the homebuyer by sharing our knowledge, expertise, and experience with them for no reason other than the intention to help them have a great homeownership experience?

Wait a minute. Are we saying that it's not enough to build a family the home they want ... now, we also have to build trust with them?

That's precisely what we're saying. Simply getting the bid and building a home is a sale. Nothing more. However, when you build trust, you create a customer.

Why is trust so important to a customer? Well, building a house is a major endeavor that can create a great deal of stress for your customer. They want to feel that they've made a good decision, one they're not going to regret. And let's not forget that as a homebuilder, you're going to spend a lot of time with this customer throughout the process. They know that you are the one who picks the people who will install the plumbing, electrical lines, and flooring. They want to know that you will only invite into their home people you trust. Their safety and investment are at stake — they have to trust that you know what you're doing, and mistakes won't jeopardize their family or their home down the line. They're going to turn to you for advice when alterations and modifications are necessary. And last, but not least, they absolutely need to trust that you'll always be working with their best interests at heart, with an unselfish intent that will leave an indelible impression.

Why is trust important to a custom builder or remodeler? First, they need to understand that it is sometimes their job to help their clients decide what they want and what they're going to get. They cannot help a customer and meet their needs if the customer can't make a decision. In addition, they need to know that they've established a mutual respect with their customers so that the normal confusion and frustrations associated with construction can be addressed during the process to keep everyone successfully working together.

Most of all, though, those in the construction industry need to diligently repair the tainted reputation that precedes us. When our customers, short-term though they might be, are asked to provide family members and friends with referrals, we want to be on the very short list. We want to create a customer experience, not a selling experience, that keeps our customers having happy ownership experiences long after we're gone.

Earning a person's trust is the highest compliment a builder can receive. When that trust is the solid foundation of your business, business will follow. People will be glad to step up and say, "If you want a homebuilder, call Ron. He won't steer you wrong."

And that, my friend, is the real difference between selling a customer and making a customer.

"Easy never produces excellence."

CHAPTER FIVE

# THE EXPERIENCE IS THE DIFFERENCE MAKER

Experience is the gateway to great relationships. The very first time you meet someone is your first experience with them. Too often, business operates from the opposite spectrum, where the first sale becomes the first experience. When you're trusting the process of building a business based on trust, the experience starts with hello, not a handshake and a signature on a dotted line.

It might be an insurance agent, the parents of your child's best friend, or even the teller at your bank. Your relationship with the person has no impact on your business, and probably never will. But did you ever pause to think that every relationship has an impact on your business? You should, because it does. And every relationship leaves behind an experience—that experience is a difference maker.

They say there is no road to happiness; happiness is the

road. It's the journey, not the destination, that is most important. If the journey is rocky, filled with disagreements about where you're going and how to get there, and wrought with detour after detour, the trip will certainly be memorable, but not enjoyable. Some might even regret they took the trip at all.

On the other hand, when a trip is enjoyable, and you find yourself in the company of people who are pleasant and helpful, you enjoy the trip—not just the destination. When you become engaged in the process, you have a stake in the outcome. The trip actually becomes an inseparable part of the entire trip, not less important or a means to an end. When people enjoy the process, they enjoy the result and become invested in it.

Have you ever had such a great experience that you couldn't wait to rave about it to everyone you knew, even if they didn't ask? That's memorable and that's a game changer. You become so invested in your experience that you relive it in every way possible and want others to share in it. It's the hallmark that many businesses strive for, but most fail to attain.

This concept was exemplified about 15 years ago, when a group of engineers were asked to improve the journey for passengers on the Eurostar. The educated answer resulted in reducing the travel time from London to Paris by 40 minutes, at a cost of six billion pounds. However, marketing expert Rory Sutherland, who is the vice-chairman of Ogilvy and Mather, believes the challenge could have been done more effectively and with a lot less money if they'd focused on improving the experience, not shortening it. His first suggestion was for Eurostar to install free Wi-Fi in its trains, which could have been done at 0.01% of the cost. His second suggestion was even more innovative, but not less effective. He proposed that they should have hired supermodels to serve as attendants, passing out free Chateau Petrus to the passengers during the journey. Both would have improved the experience for the passengers, and both would have saved tremendous amounts of money. As it was, reducing the time of the journey was quite costly, but it didn't influence the passengers' experience during the journey at all.

It is a misconception that people only care about the end result. The experience, the journey taken to get there, is equally, if not much more, important.

However, we are a society of instant gratification. Faster is better. That might be true with Internet download speeds, but it doesn't apply to everything in life, or in business for that matter. When we rush to the finish line, we sacrifice creating meaningful relationships. We might even sacrifice quality to save time. When we make it easier for ourselves, we might take the joy out of the experience for someone who has never been on this journey before.

When that happens, we invite problems. This is especially true in the building industry. Homeowners often don't know what to expect during the construction process. They have a lot of questions and many decisions to make. They're well aware of that, and that awareness brings with it expectations that their builder will walk them through the process with patience, concern, and their best interests at heart. Their builder is their saving grace and responsible for their experience. With them by their side, they know they're not on this journey alone.

Being their builder comes with responsibility. You are not only the conductor of the train, but you're also their tour guide. You're responsible for the process and the impression they have both during the journey and after they arrive to their destination. Do your customers feel like you care about your passengers, or that you only care that they paid their fare? Do your customers feel like you want them to enjoy the journey, no matter how long it lasts, or you only care about getting to the destination, the end of the project, so you can pick up another passenger and another fare?

Two skilled builders can build the very same home with the same amenities. What sets one apart from the other? The experience is the difference maker. It is the experience that the homeowner will remember long after the keys are handed over that will earn the respect, loyalty, and trust of a homeowner. An unpleasant experience will not only influence a homeowner's perception of the builder, but also of their home.

Imagine you're taking a trip to Jamaica. However, your flight was delayed due to bad weather. You slept on the floor in a crowded airport. Then, you got bumped from the first flight that went out and had to wait another day for the next one. When you finally got on the plane, your flight was full of turbulence. The flight attendants, when they could be found, were rude. The hydraulic system on the plane failed, and your landing was eventful, to say the least. Now, all of that is not likely to happen in one trip, but let's say it did. When you returned home, the last thing you ever wanted to do was go back to Jamaica. The experience took all of the joy out of the experience and it was one that you never wanted to repeat in your lifetime.

Let's look at it from another perspective. When Spirit Airlines began charging passengers for carry-on luggage, the fee wasn't part of their passengers' actual in-flight experience, but it did have an impact on their overall experience. It was a new fee that was tacked on to increase profits, although Spirit stated it would result in fewer carry-ons, which would make the boarding and deplaning process faster and would enhance safety while in flight. And, as one could expect, other airlines soon followed suit and began charging fees for carry-on baggage.

However, customers naturally perceived the additional fee negatively. They felt nickel and dimed by the airline industry, but that didn't have to happen. If the airlines had simply increased their fees by a few dollars for all passengers, the increase would have been accepted. However, by singling out those who prefer to have a carry-on on board, the passengers lacked trust in them—what would be next? Would they be charged for everything they did, even ordering tickets online or using a debit or credit card? When would the other shoe drop? They simply didn't know. With their confidence and trust waning, so did their loyalty.

It shouldn't be that way when you build a house. Sure, there will be occasions when they are delays or unexpected problems. But when you build a trusting, positive relationship, the journey can and will be pleasant, especially when the customer is already assured that their builder has no ulterior motive but to serve and help them and their builder is a person of integrity.

**Getting to Know You**

Every journey has a beginning. As a builder, the journey with your customers begins with the people you meet. From the first hello, you're leaving an impression on the people around you, long before that person might potentially become a customer. It can even begin before you meet a potential customer. Every person you meet is a potential connection to someone else who will need your services at some time in the future. What perception do they have of you? Have you given them a reason to refer you to the people they know?

When people meet you, what is their experience? Will they remember a pleasant and sincere individual who genuinely wanted to know them? Or will they recall someone who seemed busy, uninterested, or preoccupied? The people you meet become the people who share their experiences with the people they know. Remember, they are not necessarily hiring a "builder;" they are hiring a person they like and trust. In addition, they are also hiring the people you like and trust.

A contractor's experience is actually invaluable to a homeowner. They need to know that you're not only qualified, but that people they know have trusted their homes and safety to them. They need to know they're in good hands. Every builder with experience has built relationships with people in the trades—and long-term, trusting relationships with electricians, plumbers, roofers, insurance agents, suppliers, carpenters, you name it, are part and parcel of the package the homeowner gets when choosing a builder. When you have the right team and experience working together, you become even more valuable and trusted in the building industry.

Few homeowners would rush to hire a builder who lacks that experience. Even a seasoned well-running machine has an occasional wrench thrown in that throws everything off course. Inexperience exacerbates the effects and potential damage. Not only that, but a lack of experience working with suppliers and subcontractors could result in miscommunication and/or a lack of knowledge or understanding about expectations or abilities. At minimum, any of these can create discourse. The worst-case scenario could result in a total shutdown or communication and progress.

What is your experience with the people you meet *and* the people you work with? Are they pleasant and rewarding relationships that function on the basis of mutuality, where both people benefit from the relationship? What is your relationship with your employees, who are the most valuable asset a builder can have? Do they trust you? Do they trust they are going to be paid … on time? Do they trust that they have your support? Do they trust that you're making the best decisions on behalf of them and your clients? Do they trust that they'll have the tools and resources to do their job efficiently?

As a builder, you know your team is critical to your success. Their words and actions represent you and your company. There are many times when they must communicate with your clients and assist them with important decisions or explain an unexpected delay or problem. You are the pilot flying the plane, but their contributions will be noticed and become part of what will either be a positive or negative experience. Do you have a team you can trust? Have you built a relationship with qualified, experienced, and trusted individuals who mirror your core values? You should, because the people you hire will play a role in the experience you're delivering.

Think of it this way. Every experience you provide your customers will either strengthen or weaken your relationship. Your relationship with your subcontractors works on the same premise. If there isn't genuine mutual respect and trust, it will be reflected in the work they do, and it will impact their experience and the investment they should have in the process, your experience and the investment you do have, and the homeowner's experience and their level of investment in the process.

That trust has to be rebuilt with every customer and person you meet. Like Rick Warren wrote in *The Purpose Driven Life*, trust requires a track record. You cannot build trust with someone unless you have positive experiences with them. In that respect, trust requires past, present, and future experiences. Those experiences have to be replicated and not forgotten. Then, they can become a part of the overall experience that is enjoyed and admired by those you serve.

Remember, it is the journey, not the destination, that deserves your attention and focus. It is the entire journey that leaves a lasting impression and honored memories. Trust frees us up to enjoy that journey. As Goldie Hawn once wisely stated, "If we can just let go and trust that things will work out the way they're supposed to, without trying to control the outcome, then we can begin to enjoy the moment more fully. The joy of the freedom it brings becomes more pleasurable than the experience itself."

You're on the journey to build great relationships. When you make the journey more important than the destination, it will be a pleasant and amazing experience, regardless where any relationship takes you.

"Relationships, in business and life, run on the rails of trust!"

# CHAPTER SIX

# TRADITIONAL NETWORKING DOESN'T WORK

Relationships are the hallmark behind success. This is true for dentists, bankers, salespeople, and entrepreneurs in every industry. However, some people struggle with finding professional relationships. They hand out business cards, create a Facebook profile, and invest in media ads to attract customers. And then they wonder why they don't get the results they want.

For a few decades, networking has been the buzzword for business owners who want to build their clientele. Yes, most people walk into a networking event to sell, even builders. They want to find new clients, meet general contractors, and land lucrative jobs. Their intent is good, and admittedly a natural inclination, but they will never get the results they're looking for because selling doesn't work.

Their intention should be to serve. In other words, help as many people as possible without any intention of gaining work. It might sound backward, but we hold steadfast to the rule that money cannot be the ultimate goal. When done right, serving and helping will allow you to increase profits in the long run. You will be sought after and, yes, trusted far more than the company that puts in the low-dollar bid.

When you're really trying to help others and do what's best for them, the end result is growth for you and your business. When you give, it comes back to you, always. The intent cannot be based on expected returns; it should be unconditional and based on trust—trust that when you give unconditionally, it will come back to you.

It is our human nature to seek comfortable, guaranteed instant gratification. We don't want to work for it or delay that gratification for an hour, a day, a week, a month or a year! Business is results-oriented; people want a quick return on investment, even when it comes to networking. We meet people and expect the phone to start ringing, bringing us jobs right and left.

That's precisely why we get disappointed when we go to networking events and nothing happens. Let's be honest. How many of you have ever attended a networking event and walked away with a valid prospect? How many have landed a great job after shaking a hand and exchanging a business card?

That's because networking involves the wrong intent. Selling will not win over serving. Of course, everyone in the rooms knows why you're there. The problem is everyone else in the room is there for the same reason. Selfish intent has replaced the original purpose behind networking— networking is designed to share and bring value to people.

When there is no sharing and no value, there simply cannot be any benefit to the process.

One of the problems is that networking limits the time and interaction you can have with a person. You simply cannot "work the entire room" and get to know anyone with an introduction and a handshake. It's one of the biggest drawbacks to networking. Being able to meet as many people as possible in a fixed amount of time becomes the mission—not making a few quality introductions that can actually prove to be mutually beneficial. The struggle is so real that some networking events have experimented with limiting the time spent with any one individual. Like speed dating, where you meet someone and converse for a set amount of time before moving on to the next individual, human interaction has been reduced to seconds on a clock. Unfortunately, this is counterproductive to the whole intent of networking, which should be about building relationships.

Think about the last networking event you attended. Every interaction you had probably sounded like a broken record, repeated with every person you met. There's a brief introduction, followed by a handshake. Then you tell the other person what you do and hand over your business card. Moving on to the next person, you repeat the scenario. That is one of the biggest downfalls of networking, because you are telling others what you do, not why you do it.

It's the why, not the what. People are more interested in why you chose to be a builder. Why do you enjoy what you do every day? Why do you take pride in helping people design and create a home they can take pride in? It's not what you do, but why you do it, that creates an emotional attachment with people and leaves behind a positive impression.

Networking also lacks the one thing that is vital to building a business—trust. For that reason, trust requires faith—there is no immediate gratification or reward. The reward is internal. It stems from building warm, lasting, and trusting relationships.

Our clients know they can trust us—we don't sell first. We take the time to serve and help others. The natural result is that when people need anything, whether it be a general contractor or advice, they turn to us. To us, that's the greatest compliment we can receive. A business card and handshake cannot establish that type of relationship.

Oh, but what about the money? The almighty dollar that drives us to go to work every day? Well, the almighty dollar is the incentive that damages our ROI. You have to invest in your business and in every relationship before you'll begin to see any return. The short-term reward is usually the smallest and most fleeting. Think of it as disposable income—it doesn't last and has far less value than the long-term reward, which is usually a solid, stable business that is trusted by loyal clients.

Forget about getting the job. Forget about the next project coming down the pike. Forget about putting in the lowest bid and cutting costs to get the next job. Focus on the quality of relationships you make, not the quantity. Ask how you can help others and follow through, without expectation of reward, payment, or anything that might be in it for you. Forget the old adage, *I'll scratch your back if you scratch mine.*

That mindset indicates that there is an expectation of a benefit. Come from a place of sincerity, with the intention of making a valuable contribution to others. The positive energy will flow, and positive energy will come back to you. People will notice that energy. They'll naturally want to be around you. They will seek you out and ask questions. The process becomes exponential.

If people knew how powerful their thoughts and intentions were, they would activate them immediately. If you walk into a networking event with the intent to sell, people can tell. Not only will people put their guard up, but it's highly unlikely they will buy or do business with you. Some will even avoid you like the plague. That's because the intent to sell is an anti-sell virus. Selfish intent is self-sabotage. It creates results that are entirely opposite of those you want and leaves the wrong impression.

Our impressions are the ink that dyes our souls. We have to be very careful about what we allow to go into our brain, just as we have to be careful about what we put into our body. But it is no secret that it's human nature to want what is not good for us. We want to taste that which we crave — but in the end, it's not good for us. The same is true with networking. We know what we crave, and we want it *now*. But again, that's not good for us. Converting a connection into a quick sale will not build your business. It doesn't build and develop relationships. It doesn't build trust. And someday, we will look back and wonder why our business is not in a healthy state — why the foundation is crumbling, and it cannot sustain itself.

For decades, businesses have been guilty of operating from a selfish motive. For that reason, we believe that the greatest enemy for future success is past success. It's a selfish, anti-trust virus that impurifies your intent. Don't walk into a networking event to find customers! Walk in to meet people and build relationships. Trust that you will reap what you sow, rather than getting sidetracked with selfishness—don't let your ego and pride play a role in your intent or your relationships. We are susceptible to that as human beings. It's time to return to our default settings.

Most people are focused on results. We propose that people reject the result and focus instead on learning, growing, and improving. Nurture the positive energy—people are spirit, mind, and body. We are not body first. Business is the same—the results don't matter. What will matter, and impact others is the spirit and mind.

Did we just say that the results don't matter? Yes, we did. Forget about success and failure. Those are stories we tell ourselves. Thinking about results is a poison that will need to be continually fed. It's injecting yourself with something harmful to you and your business that makes you needy, addicted, if you will, on the results. And we know it doesn't work.

In fact, the top five percent of all salespeople are not results-driven. They don't focus on sales—they focus on serving and helping others. They're not selling anything—they're satisfying their customers. They're learning what their customers' needs are and focusing on how they can be of service to them. The remaining 95% of salespeople are out there pushing their products and services, lowering their price, offering incentives, making cold calls, and working ten times harder for less results.

We're working it backwards, trying to get customers first and build relationships second. That goes against our instinct, which tells us that we do business with those we know and trust. The natural chain of building relationships and trust first will produce positive results.

Do you trust the natural laws that are work? Do you trust your best to be good enough? Do you trust your own intentions to be best for you? It's a process, and before you can implement it, you must trust that it will work for you.

This is why traditional networking does not work. Relationships shouldn't be on a "what can you do for me" basis, especially when it comes to business. Think about the best relationships you've ever had—long-lasting relationships. They are based on mutual respect and infallible trust—not on the potential of benefits or money. And if money does enter the equation before that trust is built, it immediately raises concerns about whether the relationship is genuine and sincere.

Can networking work? Absolutely! When the intent is to learn, grow, and improve, but not to sell. Networking is about bringing value to others and sharing. It's not about exchanging business cards and hoping yours stands out above the rest when someone needs your services.

Let's not forget that digital relationships have taken the place of face-to-face relationships. When people want to gain customers or find a business, one of the first places they turn is to social media or the good-old-standby, Google.

There are two problems with using these types of "networking" for these purposes:

1.  Reviews from past customers or clients do not always reflect the experience with a particular business. There might have been extenuating circumstances that altered a person's perception of a company, or the reviewer is unhappy with the product they were given, not the service. For example, a reviewer may give a poor review because they regret the floor they chose in a high-traffic room, and they pass along their dissatisfaction with the business that installed that floor, even though they did an excellent job installing it.

2.  Google (and other search engines) are misleading. Every marketer strives to rank their business among the top ten in Google, where they will be seen first. Being buried at the bottom of the pile won't drive business or sales. It's all about visibility. However, being at the top of search engine results does not have any reflection on the business itself. The top-ranking businesses get there because they invest a lot of money in inching up the ranks. In addition, the businesses that pop up first might not be in the right geographical location. (In a digital world, location doesn't matter.) Those businesses might not be the most experienced or of the highest quality. This puts the businesses that might be superior at a disadvantage to those with the most money.

Yes, reviews are important. A referral is one of the best things we can earn from a customer. However, there is something even better—the referral of our peers. People who work with us in the building industry can provide educated reviews that are highly valued. They have witnessed firsthand how we treat our employees. They know whether we are reliable and professional. They know if we pay our subcontractors in full and on time. They know the quality of our craftsmanship and the rapport and respect we've earned.

You probably wouldn't entrust your loved one to just any brain surgeon or heart surgeon. If you want an opinion you can really trust, you're very likely to turn to another doctor, someone who has experience with that surgeon and knows their reputation and track record. Peer reviews are just as valuable in the building industry. For that reason, ourdesign.com was created. It's a business-to-business review site that evens the playing field. The reviews or rankings are not subject to the amount of money a business has, but instead are based on real, firsthand experience. Remember, experience is the difference maker.

Peer networking is an example of powerful networking. It is about providing credible and trusted information so that others can make credible and trusted decisions. There is no intent to sell—simply an intent to help and serve each other by providing an honest opinion and review that was earned, not bought. These peer reviews hold a great deal of power because they come from those who are highly experienced and qualified to post a review. It should be noted that past customers are not qualified to post a review.

They are not educated in the trade, whether it is carpentry or roofing. They have little or nothing to compare their experience to, and their review is usually biased. When professional peer reviews are favorable, it is usually because the reviewer is educated and experienced with the company. Above all, there is no selling, expectation, or intent. The sole purpose is to contribute something of value to a network of professionals in the trade—our trusted opinion.

Trusted opinions have more value than a $500 newspaper advertisement. To a business owner, trusted opinions are priceless. They are the calling card that builds a track record of success and are much more effective than the exchanging business cards game in networking events.

When we remove any intent to sell and instead focus our time, attention, and effort on building relationships, we find that we don't have to sell at all. If we build relationships, the business will come. It's part of the natural laws. When we build relationships, we don't have to network. Referrals will come. It's part of the natural process. When we build relationships, we don't have to reduce our prices or create incentives. People will forget about low bids and instead seek a builder they can trust, and they will pay for the reassurance that they have found a builder who is qualified, skilled, experienced, highly recommended, and who genuinely cares about them.

Therein lies the answer. The days when a business was authentic and sincere are long gone. Customers do not believe companies care about them at all. They are skeptical of their motives and believe that are considered prospects, not valued people.

Whether you are marketing yourself or your company, make sure there are no strings attached. It should never be about what's in it for you, but always about what's in it for the people you're helping.

The next time you're networking, approach it with a different mindset—to help others *unconditionally*. Have absolutely no preset expectations or hopes. Walk in with an open mind and a positive attitude. For every minute you talk business with someone, spend ten minutes talking about other things.

Wait, that doesn't sound like business! Its sounds like making friends based on mutual interests and respect. Bingo! That's your intent. Nothing more. You might not walk out with a brand-new customer or a lead on a new project. But you will walk out with relationships and friendships that are based on trust. Every one of those relationships is a new opportunity, full of golden nuggets that would have never come your way if you'd spent all of your time and effort looking for them.

# Moore's Law Of Achievement

## Attitudes + Skills + Actions = Results

1 + 1 + 1 = 3...You can't change the 3, without changing the 1's!

# Moore's Path To Peak Performance

| Learn | Grow | Improve |
|---|---|---|
| Attitudes | Skills | Actions |
| Likable | Trustworthy | Expert |
| Helpful | Caring | Courageous |

Your 'To Be List' will help you keep score of the right things!

CHAPTER SEVEN

# BREAKTHROUGHS AND TRANSFORMATIONS ... IT'S NEVER TOO LATE TO GET IT RIGHT

S
o, you're a builder. For years, you've been working under the bid and build concept. Sometimes you win; sometimes you lose. That's the nature of bids—the best builder might not get the job, but the lowest bidder often does. The truth is, placing bids to get business is a gamble, and it's one only one bidder can win for each project. There are always more losers than there are winners.

There is nothing wrong with relying on bids to get contracts. It's how this industry works and has worked for decades. Unfortunately, we know that the three-bid process doesn't work and is not an indication of a builder's skill, experience, or reputation. In addition, it's a concept that relies on money, which is no different than a sales script on a price tag—it's all about the money. And let's not forget one important factor—if a customer only solicits three bids, that automatically puts many builders out of contention.

This book proposes another strategy—build trust first. Forget about bids, marketing, and selling. With trust as your solid foundation, you will get better results that will last long after any project ends. For those who are new to the industry, it's a strategy you can begin to employ from the onset. Get to know people and serve them. Find out what they like and what interests them. Make an effort to assist them when you can and form a mutual friendship. When they are ready to build, or know someone who is, yours will be the first name that comes to mind. Because they know and respect you, they'll want to recommend you to the people they know and respect. What goes around, indeed, does come around.

But what if you've been in business for years and are cemented in the bid process to gain work? Does this concept even apply to you? We are adamant that, yes, it does. In fact, this puts you in a position where you can gauge the results, compared to the bid and build process.

Here is another reason why builders should incorporate trust into their brand. We know that many of the processes in construction are centered around technical management. However, the industry has neglected to acknowledge that social factors have a huge impact on our trade. You can juggle numbers from one line item to another all day, but you also need to understand that trust has a significant effect on project efficiency and teamwork. When trust is low on a project, there will be decreased efficiency and, likely, increased administrative oversight and costs. Trust is also the primary driver in subcontractor selection, a relationship that is imperative to the success of every project.

We also know that basing your business on a strong foundation of trust requires faith. But when you became a builder, you had that same faith—faith that you would build a strong reputation and successful business. Still, you might struggle to find work, get invitations to bid, get more bids accepted, and gain referrals. If that's the case and you're like many in your boots, you're still waiting for your lucky break—you know that break, the one that you've worked so hard for that will open the flood gates and get your business on a solid and consistent footing.

Here's a news flash! You don't need a break. You need a breakthrough. Doing the same thing over and over will only produce the same results you've been getting. In order to get the change, you're seeking, you have to change.

Businesses changes all of the time. In fact, change is vital to the success of every business in every industry. Advances in technology drive change, as do social trends. Public priorities also change over time, and what was once considered non-negotiable can become a thing of the past with the passing of just one event that puts things into a different perspective. There are always trends in business, and today's customer definitely seeks more than qualified professionals—they want to employ people and businesses they can trust.

Change also applies to business models. The way we used to do business, with a handshake and a person's word, has been replaced with detailed contracts, reduced costs, and the desire to increase profits. With those changes came the need for greater oversight and the word so many love to hate: micromanagement. Naturally, micromanaged employees don't feel trusted and are, therefore, less productive, less efficient, and more likely to leave for greener pastures. It's also true that employees who don't feel trusted are not likely to trust their managers.

Yes, trust begets trust. If you sincerely trust a person, they are more likely to trust you. In the building industry, you have to trust your employees, supplier, subcontractors, and all of the rest of the parts of the machine that must work together to complete a major project on time and within budget. When you display that trust, all of the agents working together will trust you in return. They will work harder and be willing to expend extra effort when it is needed. They'll also be more likely to step up to the plate and be problem solvers, helping you by troubleshooting and seeking solutions when a problem or delay arises.

This level of trust requires transparency. The good thing about transparency is that it can become a policy, regardless how old a business is. The more your employees and subcontractors, suppliers, etc., know about you and your business, the more likely it is that they will be assured that they know enough about you to trust you. When information is not disclosed, on the other hand, people often wonder why … and they assume it's because there is something you don't want them to know.

The fact is, there are so many more pros than cons when considering building a platform and reputation based on trust. This extends beyond you, the owner and contractor. Everyone in your office and on a job-site represents you, the contractor. This includes the person who answers your telephone and the different trades—carpenters, drywallers, plumbers, electricians, roofers, painters, etc.—they are all your voice to homeowners, code inspectors, and the public. With so many roles involved in the building process, it is vital that you trust that they know their job and will do it, which is precisely what your customers want from you— they want to know that you have the experience, skill, relationships, and team to provide them with quality work. If you bid the job, you were only talking the talk. On the job site, you must walk the walk.

In this book's introduction, we discussed how a lack of trust torpedoed a relationship. Once it started to crumble, it avalanched into a catastrophe that couldn't be repaired. So, too, is the case in your building business. If you do not build your business on a strong and solid foundation, it will weaken over time. Eventually, it might not be strong enough to sustain itself. If you want something to last, it must have a good foundation. As they say, churches have large foundations ... outhouses don't.

Our reputation in the community is something we can control. We know that we cannot control the economy. We know we cannot control interest rates or lending criteria. We know we cannot govern the current prevailing rate of pay of the tradespeople, just as we are powerless to control the costs of building supplies and delivery fees. We can only build them into the cost of doing business. We cannot control our competition, their Google ranking, or their fixed bid price. But we can control the relationships we build with every sector of our businesses. We can control the timeline in which we pay our suppliers, subcontractors, and employees. We can control the safety of the workplace, and we can control the work culture for everyone involved. That includes the homeowner who will inevitably spend a considerable amount of time on site. Above all, we can control our honor and our word. In fact, we are the only ones with the power to do so.

While it is easiest to build trust first and build our business on that foundation later, any business, regardless of its age, can begin to make trust a priority. Yes, even weak foundations can be repaired or rebuilt.

The transformation begins with you. You are the face of your business with everyone you meet. Operate from a place of integrity and sincerity. Do what you say and say what you'll do. Surprises are great when they involve celebrations, but they are rarely applauded or appreciated in the building process.

And don't forget, advice is free—don't withhold it from someone in need. When you build a business model, you're not selling yourself or your business. So, there is no need to feel like you're giving anything away. It costs you nothing to let people know that you care, and by offering much-needed advice to an individual, you'll gain not only a friend, but someone who will refer you to their friends. And there is another bonus—the person you advise is likely to be qualified and experienced in a different field or industry. Someday, you may value their opinion and advice, as well.

We've talked about trusting your employees and subcontractors. You know them and their capabilities. You also want them to trust you and know that you're looking out for their safety, wellbeing, and success. But what happens when you find you don't know a person well enough to know if they're trustworthy or not?

There will be times when you will be called upon to trust someone you don't know. In that case, do due diligence. You wouldn't want to give the person access to your bank accounts, but you should be able to ascertain whether the individual has earned the trust of others.

If you're still reluctant to strengthen your brand through trust, let's address some potential concerns:

1. Risk aversion: Many business owners don't like to take risks. While trust is a trait that does involve change, it doesn't involve risk. There is no financial investment or loss. In fact, being trustworthy cannot depreciate a reputation; it can only make a reputation more valuable. In other words, there is everything to gain, but nothing to lose.

2. You don't like change. Well, neither did Blockbuster. They rented movies out of their brick-and-mortar stores, and they were hell bent on that business model. Their reluctance to change resulted in their demise. Change is necessary, and when change doesn't involve risk (see #1 above), there is every reason to consider it.

3. You're a builder, not a social person. You do what you know and know what you do. That's great!

However, in business, as it is in life, you have to communicate and interact with people on a daily basis. You don't have to be outgoing and highly social to sincerely help others and conduct yourself and your business with integrity. Trust has nothing to do with charm—snake oil salesmen had charm, but they weren't trustworthy. Trust, however, has everything to do with intent. It's also important to remember what your customer wants. Today's customer looks beyond skills and experience, preferring to do business with people and companies that are transparent, socially responsible, and concerned about their economic footprint. These are all soft skills, and trust plays a vital role in them.

It's never too late to get it right. Every person you meet is a new beginning, and every new customer is a new opportunity to strengthen your brand and solidify your reputation as a person of integrity, authenticity, and sincerity. It's a transformation that will last long after the job is done, but one that will plant a seed that will bear fruit for years to come.

"Without a higher purpose, we are left with only a selfish one."

# CHAPTER EIGHT

# TRUST—THE FOUNDATION OF ALL GOOD THINGS

There is more to life than us. There is more to life than a sale. No matter what your faith is, trust that there is a higher purpose.

We have to trust that which we cannot see. It is important to trust yourself, the process, and others. Without those things, no matter what you build in life, you will never build anything that lasts, whether it is an idea, an intention, a building, or a relationship.

Pure intentions are part of the process. Whenever any person is taking advantage of others, they set a process in motion that cannot sustain long-term success. Sure, short-term success is possible, but the real, valuable, permanent success can only survive if it is infused with and based on trust.

In this book, you've met living examples of trust—they are pillars in our industry and their communities who represent the values, characteristics, and principles in this book. We applaud them and happily accept their contribution to this book. You might also notice that we use the word "love" in describing our relationships. That is intentional.

Every relationship in life stems from love—love for companionship, love for partners, love for our customers and love for our employees. That loves removes selfish intent and replaces it with authenticity, genuineness, and a mutual trust that is always reciprocated ... never violated.

The one thing that separates us from automation is our emotional capacity. We can feel, we can love, and we can forgive others. Machines and technology cannot replicate the huge advantage that the human element brings to business, and those things never will.

We've all met people who have a salesman smile, and we can immediately sense that it is fake. They seem to be lacking that genuine human element that draws people to each other. It's that feeling that we get—*I don't know what it is about that person, but I don't trust them.* That's preconscious communication. Our brain takes it in, and at the brain stem, it is interpreted—not because of anything that is said but based on nonverbal signals. It is so true that our intent cannot be faked ... or hidden. Our intentions are louder than words. It is also true that our actions come from our intentions.

At the business level, a selfish intention outweighs all of our behavior. That's because our greatest human power is our intentions. Without pure intentions to unconditionally care and trust that we invest in others and give unconditionally, the results will come and multiply. On the other hand, if we operate on selfish intent in business, we will be doomed, and we will be replaced by automation and machines that provide better service.

We have to learn to do what is best for each other, without any desire for a return. Doing what is best for the customer doesn't mean giving people what they want but giving people what is best for them. That is a solid foundation for business, just as it is for life.

The human factor relies on trust. It puts people first. Companies cannot get better unless they help their people get better. Companies cannot be their best unless they do what is best for their customers. We have to grow and improve at a higher level—only then can we build a foundation that is solid and worthy of supporting a substantial business and a substantial life.

In this book, you've met real like-minded examples of people who live by this principle. Our relationships with them are solid because they are built on a strong foundation of trust. These are the top five percenters—the people who trust the process and understand that trust is the most valuable asset in business and in life.

Every relationship, whether it is professional or personal, should be built on a foundation that is strengthened by these principles. Unfortunately, too many have been weakened because profits have been prioritized over people. Any weakness causes instability and a foundation that cannot support growth. We've witnessed many businesses come and go because their foundations are not strong enough to stand the test of time.

Let's stop looking for the hidden or missing key to success. It's always been here; it's just been forgotten. It is about doing what is right, for no other reason than the fact that it is the right thing to do.

At the beginning of this book, we said that it's time to take business back to a handshake. However, we are always evolving. Throughout the process of writing this book, we have grown. We have learned. We have improved, and we now know that business doesn't need to return to a handshake. It needs to evolve from a handshake to a hug.

"Profits are seeds.

Don't spend them…

Plant them."

# Real Stories...Living Examples

## JOHN WALLACE

### FOUNDER OF JW FLOORING, RE:SOURCE FLOORS, JW CLEANING & RESTORATION, AND OUTREACH IMPACTING LIVES

### TRUST AND VERIFY

I met John Wallace because of another relationship I had made over 20 years before I met him. The first thing about John that comes to mind is that one of the many benefits of good relationships is that they attract more good relationships. That said, John built JW Floor Covering, Re:Source Floors and JW Cleaning & Restoration on a foundation of relationships built on trust and a commitment to serving people.

Many people make that statement, but John lives with that purpose. He serves others and trusts that every good thing comes from loving, respecting and caring for people. John's commitment to these values touch his family, friends, employees, customers, vendors, suppliers, and finally his community – and make no mistake, John believes the whole world is his community. He established Outreach Impacting Lives as a vehicle to help those who haven't found the truth in life to set them free, those who are struggling, and those who need to experience love in action.

John has made giving hope, assistance, and love to others one of his daily responsibilities.

He puts doing what's best for people before making a profit but understands making profits helps him serve people. John is an exceptional business leader who pays close attention to his businesses. He's just always aware if the profit isn't right, it's because people aren't being treated properly. When John errs, he errs on the side of second chances. He has and will always be committed to serving people and does this daily by growing relationships built on trust. One of his favorite statements is, "Trust and Verify." This exemplifies his desire to trust people and his understanding they need leadership, guidance, and encouragement to be their best! John has developed the next generation of leadership at Re:Source Floors in principals Jeff Floodberg and Brittany Purdy, at JW Floor Covering in executives Chris Tiffany and Dean Bednar and JW Cleaning & Restoration executive Joe Kovacs. All are building on the lessons they have learned working with John. I expect that the long-term outlook for these companies will be bright.

# JOE LAUTNER
# NORTEK SECURITY & CONTROL

## SERVING RELATIONSHIPS
## BY BEING A TRUSTED ADVISOR

Changing paradigms in any market can require a business or even an industry to take a giant leap of faith and trust that what they are about to do will be best for everyone involved. That's exactly what Nortek Security & Control did. In the high-volume 'New Home' market, successfully building and delivering new homes requires a tight process and change is met with scrutiny as the cost of delays and any added expense can damage reputation and profits. Smart Homes are an exploding trend, and new home builders know they their buyers want solutions. However, they are not sure where to start.

Nortek Security & Control, launched the ELAN New Home Program specifically to address the needs of the new home market. For over 25 years, Nortek has delivered Security, Entertainment, and Home Control solutions working through home-technology installers. ELAN is its premier home automation and control brand. With the growth in connected home demand, NSC knew they needed to do more to help the builders and capitalize on this opportunity.

In the first year, they studied the high-volume new home market to really learn what problems builders faced and developed a program to meet their needs. What they learned, basically, is that builders want to sell more homes and create happy customers. In other words, builders want solutions, not products. NSC's 'ELAN New Home Program' delivers a compelling Smart & Connected Home solution AND provides direct manufacturer system design, builder-sales team training, and 'sell-thru' marketing support so the builder maximizes their investment, differentiates their development, and sells more homes.

I met Joe Lautner, VP of Strategic Solution for NSC, at an industry event. NSC had been selling home technology through their professional install channel working with builders but in a supporting role through their install partner. "We provided great support to our customers but knew we could do more. Our installer-customers are small businesses without deep marketing teams and other business development resources," Joe said. "By developing a program that educated builders and delivered turn-key solutions with the marketing and sales support, we helped our dealers be better at supporting their builder relationships. And we became a valuable resource to builders by helping them understand the connected home space and delivering a turn-key connected home solution with a qualified installer who could support them." NSC set out to build trust and help their customers, and that's what they're doing.

Today, the ELAN New Home Program is delivering value to both their professional installers and to builders. "What started out as an effort to grow connected home product sales in the high-volume builder market has developed into much more," Joe now says with confidence. "We are a trusted advisor to both our integrator customers and the builder. Our integrators trust us, so they invite us to their builder meetings, and we help them better serve their builder relationships. Builders work with us because we take the mystery out of the connected home space, deliver complete and compelling solutions, provide direct oversight, and have a great network of professional installers to keep them on scheduling—selling more homes."

# COREY BRUSHIA

# FOUNDER AND PRESIDENT OF ONE TOUCH LIVING

## CREATING A CULTURE OF ACCOUNTABILITY

Corey Brushia is the owner and founder of One Touch Living, a lifestyle electronics and home automation system business that also provides hospitality and commercial audio visual systems.

He is passionate about what he does and has always led with the idea that doing a good job is the best marketing. By doing what is right by his clients, Corey has never had to market or advertise his business. Corey credits his success with creating a company culture that focuses on both his team and his customers.

"It is the team that you have around you, the people around you, and the other contractors on the job," Corey said. "It starts with the culture that you build within your company."

"When you are meeting with a potential client and building that trust in a relationship if you come from an authentic place it just shows through. That is the only real sales that you need."

Corey explained that his company just went through a significant remodel and he has interviewed a lot of different contractors. It became readily apparent when he encountered those who weren't truthful or were not authentic to having their best interests at heart.

Corey states that, "The only good deal is a mutual deal where everybody benefits."

"We have been around since 2000, and I have brought on strategic partners and actual partners. My core employees have been with me since the beginning. Everyone in the company has become a family."

To create that type of culture, Corey states that it is necessary to be careful when you are in transition and hiring people. One wrong person can become a cancer and it trickles down to the customer.

On the other hand, Corey says that when your employees are happy, everyone is on the same page and fighting the same fight. They become excited about how things are going. As a result, business will naturally come.

"This culture affords you the ability to not have to take on clients who you don't want," he explained, "and to really focus on the clients and projects that are beneficial and that you can be proud of. From the initial meeting, when you take that approach with clients, you are not selling anymore. You are always selling yourself; you are not selling your products."

"It starts with leadership. You can't rule with an iron fist. We are all accountable to one another. If one of us drops the ball our accountability is our guilt because we dropped the ball and let our teammates down. That accountability to one another creates a different kind of relationship. Everyone seems to rise to the occasion, and everyone goes above and beyond.

When we asked Corey, what trust means to him, he offered the following definition:

"Trust is intangible and tangible. It is a feeling of assurance you have earned ... and can easily lose. It is the most valuable commodity on earth. Trust is a faith and a belief in yourself and in others."

Corey has created a culture within One Touch Living that values trust. He also values his employees. However, he admits that there will be problems in a business, but it is their perspective that makes a difference.

"One of the things we instill in our employees and as a culture is that our company and employees believe that problems are not problems. They are opportunities to shine. By approaching a problem with the right attitude and overcoming that problem, that is where you set yourself apart."

By creating a culture of trust and accountability, Corey has set One Touch Living apart from the rest. For his clients and employees, it is a culture where everybody benefits. As a result, he can focus on selling his company, without having to sell at all.

# RANDY AND DEBBIE WISE
# RANDY WISE HOMES

## BE YOUR BEST TO HELP OTHERS BE THEIR BEST

I met Randy and Debbie Wise because of the age we live in. That's right, if it weren't for the power of social media, I would probably have never met them. We connected on Facebook and after following each other long enough to build trust that we shared a belief in helping and serving people, we connected in person and became friends.

Randy and Debbie own Randy Wise Homes in Niceville, Florida. Yep, that's right, Niceville, and it had to be divine intervention that placed them in a town named for how they behave. They grew up there, and they live in a way that proves they believe that love is the greatest power, even in business. They have been loving the people in the Northwest part of Florida and making customers – not just sales – for decades. They are on a mission to be their best by helping others be their best!

Their pursuit of excellence is the starting point for all their relationships and makes them trustworthy and being trustworthy makes their business grow. This philosophy put into action has made their lives rich with purpose. They count serving their family, friends, employees, customers and community a privilege.

Randy once said to me, "Business runs on the rails of relationships!" Now, if that doesn't exemplify understanding that building trust first is the best business practice, I don't know what does.

Randy and Debbie have a passion for homebuilding and a commitment to giving back to their community. There seems to always be a great sense of gratitude in anyone who has the understanding that relationships, people, and trust are the foundation of all good things, and they exemplify this in all they do. One of the examples of this is their involvement in Building Homes for Heroes to honors those who have served.

In an age when people are easily frustrated and blame others, Randy and Debbie Wise take responsibility for their actions and show respect for others in their personal and business lives. The Randy Wise Homes leadership team of Caleb Wise, Steve Thomas and Luke Philpott are exceptional leaders who make the future of Randy Wise Homes look like more of the same love and care for its employees, customers and community.

# LAWRENCE W. CERENZIE M.S.
## PRESIDENT AND CHEMICAL ENGINEERING MANAGER, FSC COATINGS, INC.

### TRUST: "THE" KEY COMPONENT TO FSC COATINGS, INC. OPERATIONS, VISION AND LOGO MISSION STATEMENT

From our inception in 1986, FSC Coatings, Inc. had a "VISION" that is imbedded in our company logo: **"Coatings Engineered for Ultimate Performance."** Hence, FSC's Vision meant our focus was to build and supply the highest performance coatings, paints, waterproofing systems, and wood finishes available anywhere. While the big boxes and major paint companies have gone to producing low cost systems with low initial installed cost, we have taken the opposite approach believing that people really want their investments to last the very longest for each dollar spent. And this is how it all started...

After graduating with my chemical engineering degree from LSU, I went to work for ARCO Oil & Gas's Materials Engineering Research & Development Team with a focus on Coatings/Paints Research and Testing. In the oil, gas, and chemical world, extended paint and coating longevity means lives saved, environmental damage eliminated, and structures protected in that they can continue to function as designed. From this experience, came our VISION of making and selling the longest lasting systems available anywhere.

My brother and partner, Dr. Steve Cerenzie, has a biochemical engineering background with a healthcare field doctorate. Steve's technical background plus construction experience with Navy Ships and oilfield construction in harsh environments (as with Alaska's Prudhoe Bay Oilfield development) is critical to understanding common construction and application issues.

Life Cycle costs are always the ultimate measure of cost effectiveness. In 1979, ARCO performed a unique study of actual costs of using only "the best" versus using the second and third best performing systems. There was always pressure from the purchasing department to approve as many systems as possible, so they could get "the lowest price" possible for any project. What the engineering team found was that it was always "CHEAPEST" to use the #1 performing product versus the runners-up in terms of life cycle costs. They found that uptime was increased, maintenance in hostile (and expensive environments) minimized and project lives extended when the #1 performing product was used, of which paints and coatings were one of the categories. Given that the projects included ranged from Louisiana to Texas offshore/offshore to California offshore/onshore to Alaska's very difficult Cook Inlet offshore (2nd highest tides in the world) to Alaska's North Slope, this effort covered many different kinds of operating environments. But after a few years of evaluation, it was clear that using the #1 rated product in each category provided maximum returns, highest levels of uptime, highest levels of safety for man & the environment and lowest Life Cycle Costs.

As to paints and coatings specifically, it meant one manufacturer was ahead of the rest and received all of ARCO's major project business. That unique position gave them some pricing power, but it also assured us of the longest lasting systems possible in any environment ...whether low corrosion rates or the most hostile environments. It meant we literally built a partnership of sorts with that company...and they never let us down.

Our big issue then was quality control of the applications and selecting the very best applicators to assure that the maximum longevity was achieved. Of the hundreds of projects with coatings issues reported, only ONE was an actual failure of the system...the rest were ALL applicator errors of one sort or another. The TRUST earned only deepened over time...they did not let us down.

This was a very interesting lesson that I have never forgotten and has guided our "VISION" and work at FSC Coatings over the last 30 years. For us, when people specify and buy our systems, they place TRUST in us and our products...that we will protect their valuable assets and treasures better and longer than anyone else. The vast majority of our customers are "Repeat Customers" making TRUST in us and our systems our most valuable commodities.

And that particular Ultra-Performance Acrylic topcoat that ARCO specified exclusively for many years for the Trans Alaskan Pipeline, ARCO's Offshore platforms and the

North Slope Oil Production Facilities is what we now call our Bio-Safe MaxLife Coatings System. Working with our trusted manufacturing partner of 30 years, we modified that original metal coating system to "breathe" to make it functional for wood, stucco, block and other architectural surfaces. The process took some work, but we carefully modified the system to be more flexible and allow "entrained moisture" (from condensation in the walls, roofing leaks, moist substrates that were coated while "wet", plumbing/piping that "sweats", etc.) to escape the coating film without disbonding or bubbling. Our first major world-class project was in the San Francisco PIER-waterfront tourist area utilizing these modified systems wherein we finished #1 in their three-year test program against many major U.S. national and regional paint companies. To make things more difficult, the wood siding was about 100 years old on average...and fully covered with mold, mildew and fungus of varying colors and textures.

The results? The maintenance folks were historically painting the San Francisco Pier project every 1 to 1.5 years with common premium paints and stains which was a major cost and safety issue for the PIER management team. The safety and lawsuit concerns were exacerbated given they have over 10 Million visitors per year...and the repaint and repair work had to be done while the PIER was in full operation.

Enter FSC Coating's systems, the Bio-Safe MaxLife Ultra-Performance Paints was not redone until over 10 years had lapsed since application. And after that 10+ year exposure period, the PIER Project wood, galvanized and masonry surfaces looked essentially perfect to everyone. What was especially amazing was that many of those wood and masonry surfaces actually take "full wave action" during larger storms...a pretty tough proposition when dealing with wood and masonry surfaces. With organic growth having been a huge issue before with the 100-year-old wood, the specialized Bio-Safe® Prime & Seal® and Super Prime Stain Blocking Primers operated flawlessly. The Bio-Cleaner was important in being able to clean the salt and spore laden surfaces without any environmental or applicator health concerns. Not only was the adhesion perfect, but there was not one show of visible mold, fungus or mildew anywhere on the nearly 800,000 square feet of wood-sided and masonry surfaces.

The specialized TWP® Natural Wood Systems made for the PIER Project were redone after 5 to 7 years with other competitors not even making one year. The AWR Super Sealer road and pavement sealing system had to hold up to routine daily steam cleaning...and it lasted over 5 years with almost 1 million people per month walking on them, cars driving on them, delivery trucks driving on them and food exposure galore.

A NYSE property management firm (over 200 shopping centers and commercial facilities) operating mostly on the East and Gulf Coasts, decided to evaluate paint longevity. After 10 years of side by side testing and full project applications, they determined that our Bio-Safe MaxLife Ultra Performance Paint systems saved them between 30 and 70% on Life Cycle Costs for siding, stucco, metal roofing, metal railings and so forth. It was very gratifying when they invited us to the presentation of that data to their regional operations managers. Again, it was proof that making the very best does build TRUST and leads to long term relationships that are good for the manufacturer, supplier, specifier, applicator and end-use customer.

From these development and project testing efforts, FSC Coatings' reputation began to grow and with it came TRUST that actually transferred to more customers, architects, engineering firms, military branches, water districts and energy companies across the U.S. FSC's Bio-Safe® MaxLife Coating System has been used extensively to restore major shopping centers, military facilities, historic monuments in Alaska, Cape Canaveral projects, **a high profile Los Angeles area Museum (exterior surfaces including mile long walls along I-405 and much of the interior)**, Coast Guard Light Houses, difficult military kitchens, La Jolla's VA Hospital, the LDS Church's Orlando Temple, church buildings, major Health & Fitness Center locations including dressing rooms & pool areas, numerous University of California facilities, recoating of major shopping center roofs, island projects, various restaurant projects and so on. For the residential builder and owner, it has meant true waterproofing systems with very long life at a very reasonable cost...the LOWEST Life Cycle Cost system on the market and a very easy system to maintain when the time for recoating comes.

Following is a Rancho Santa Fe home that was coated with our Bio-Safe® MaxLife Coating System after 15+ years of exposure. This home was coated by Jack Corvin of Corvin

Painting ... an excellent example of the performance that is possible with the best coating systems applied by the highest quality level applicators.

And the picture proves our point of what is possible when the "vision" of building the very best is totally embodied by supplier and manufacturers as the means to earn the long-term TRUST of our customers.

(Note: the natural finish garage doors are finished with our 400 Series System at about 4 years)

# WILLIAM MARSHALL
# DOMESTIC FAB DESIGN STUDIO

## YOU ARE GOOD ENOUGH—TRUST YOURSELF

After working tirelessly to accomplish the major milestones in his life—graduating from college, going through the military, landing his first big job—each time he would go to the most important person in his life to share it with… or at least the person he was seeking the most approval from … and each time he was denied that feeling of approval, that moment to have someone, the person that mattered most, be truly proud of him for his achievements was taken away…..That person was his father

Because of those moments of denial, he has spent his life over compensating. His accomplishments which are already amazing, occasionally get embellished when telling others about them. He was hurt before, and he will not take that chance again…He doesn't believe that the amazing things that he is doing are good enough… the worst mistrust of all is not trusting himself… not trusting that he is good enough.

Will is constantly donating his time, money, and resources to serve others … giving himself tirelessly to people who probably don't deserve it, always going the extra mile to prove that he is worthy to be their friend, partner, employee, salesman…

Even though he was handed the highest award in his field of expertise in his industry, by his peers in the industry, part of him still believes that he is not worthy. When being given his award for Best Salesman of the Year, his acceptance speech was more than humble ... he thanked everyone around him for being the reason that he was there. He even thanked someone for helping him with the words to say while he was actually giving the speech.

The truth is he is great all on his own... his humbleness inspires others. He is the best salesman of the year because he has never sold anything to anyone; he just helps them as a friend. Bending over backwards to make sure they are happy, he does everything possible to seek their approval and fill a void that was left by someone who was probably not worthy of his trust... to trust that they would give him the approval and validation that everyone deserves in that moment.

Now Will's biggest challenge is not to earn other people's trust because he is truly amazing and everyone around him trusts him ... his challenge is to trust himself—to trust that he is worthy of other people's trust and that he is good enough ... to trust the process.... and if he falls short in any way, that those closest to him will understand and will still believe in him and they will still love him. He is now looking forward to enjoying the journey... and sharing his story was his first step in choosing to enjoy the journey.

# MEET THE AUTHOR

# RON BLACKBURN

Ron Blackburn is a serial entrepreneur, inventor, innovator, author, founder and CEO of several companies built around the building industry. He is a board member of 19 non-profits nationally and internationally. He is a board member of Karma International, President of the San Diego Chapter, and is an Honorary Sheriff for the San Diego Deputy Sheriffs Association. Within the building industry, Ron sits on two boards and chairs several committees for the San Diego Building Industry Association.

Ron is a developer, custom homebuilder, subcontractor, material and safety product supplier, architect, and consultant. He handles all phases of building and has 40 years' experience in the industry. Ron is also the founder and CEO of OurDesign, a relationship oriented, interactive B2B Platform and mobile app for the building industry. Ron has a passion for connecting people and building relationships and believes that all of our successes in life are built on trust. When we connect with people, we create relationships. Relationships build Trust ... and with Trust, we can build anything!

To contact Ron Blackburn, visit www.OurDesign.com. Email Ron at Ron@Ourdesign.com.

# MEET THE AUTHOR

# MIKE MOORE

M ike Moore is a people builder whose passion is developing leaders who coach and managers who mentor and he is obsessed with helping people pursue excellence!

Mike is a featured keynote speaker, author, leadership, peak performance and sales performance coach. He believes we were each created to be exceptional but are held back by our default human settings that cause people to be average. He has dedicated his life to learning how to reset his own and help others rest these default setting to live to their highest self and reach their peak performance.

He was raised to coach, teach, and lead by his father, a coach, and his mother, a teacher, and is a lifelong student of leadership, coaching, team building, peak performance and the profession of sales.

Mike's been speaking, writing, training and coaching professionally since 1992 and has created keynotes, presentations, courses, workshops, seminars, breakout and coaching sessions that now make up his MOORE LEADERSHIP & PEAK PERFORMANCE SERIES. In his sessions, he shares unique insights from some of the greatest coaches of all time and how to apply them to business. By doing this, he teaches leaders and managers how to coach, set standards and instill a performance culture where people thrive, and profits are a result, not the focus.

Mike is a lifelong learner who inspires and motivates people to become people who are constantly learning, growing, and improving.

He has developed THE MAKING CUSTOMERS SERIES from his 42 years of experience in Retailing, Homebuilding, Design Centers and Floor Covering to address the specific challenges faced every day by owners, executives, managers and employees in these industries. Mike is a people builder who believes all good things begin with trust, so trust is the foundation for all good things.

Mike is also considered a futurist who began speaking about the Internet, technology and the 'new economy' in 1994. In 1996, he co-founded and developed Options Online, an award-winning Online Design Studio and Options Operating System for the Homebuilding Industry, which is now available as Studio Chateau and has grown to process over 2 billion dollars annually. Today, he continues to help owners, executives, managers and salespeople address the challenges of this 'new economy'.

Contact Mike Moore by sending an email to mmoore@makingcustomers.com.